Beginner's Guitar for Kids

with Winden and Squiggy

Written by Corey Klaus

Illustrations by Pamela Hodges

nepeta

NEPETA ENTERPRISES LLC

POTTSTOWN

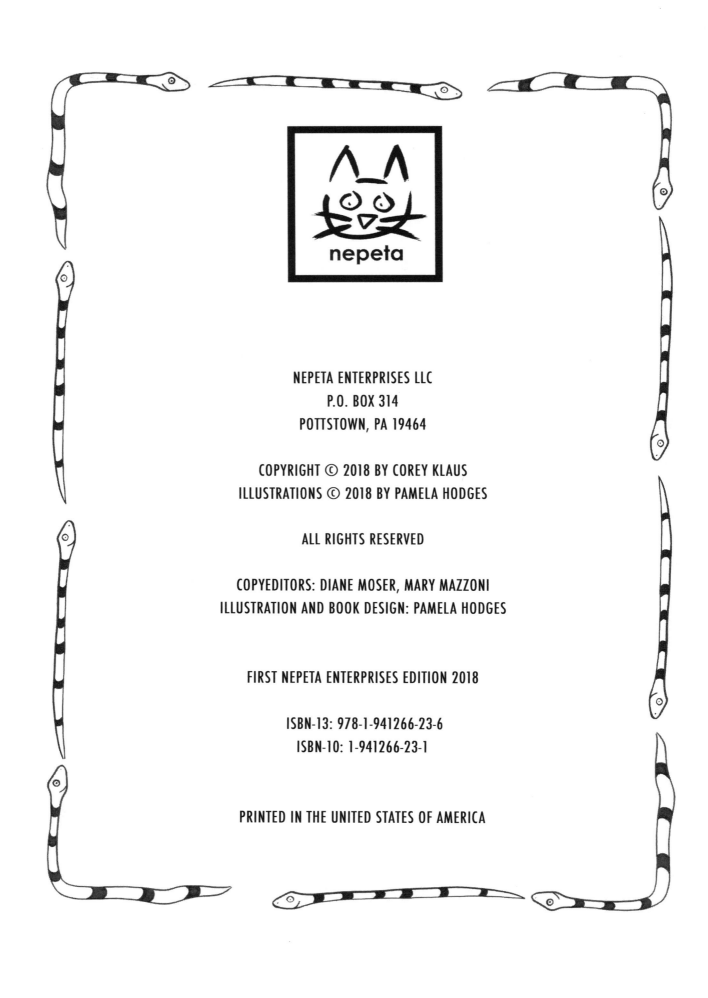

nepeta

NEPETA ENTERPRISES LLC
P.O. BOX 314
POTTSTOWN, PA 19464

COPYEDITORS: DIANE MOSER, MARY MAZZONI
ILLUSTRATION AND BOOK DESIGN: PAMELA HODGES

FIRST NEPETA ENTERPRISES EDITION 2018

ISBN-13: 978-1-941266-23-6
ISBN-10: 1-941266-23-1

PRINTED IN THE UNITED STATES OF AMERICA

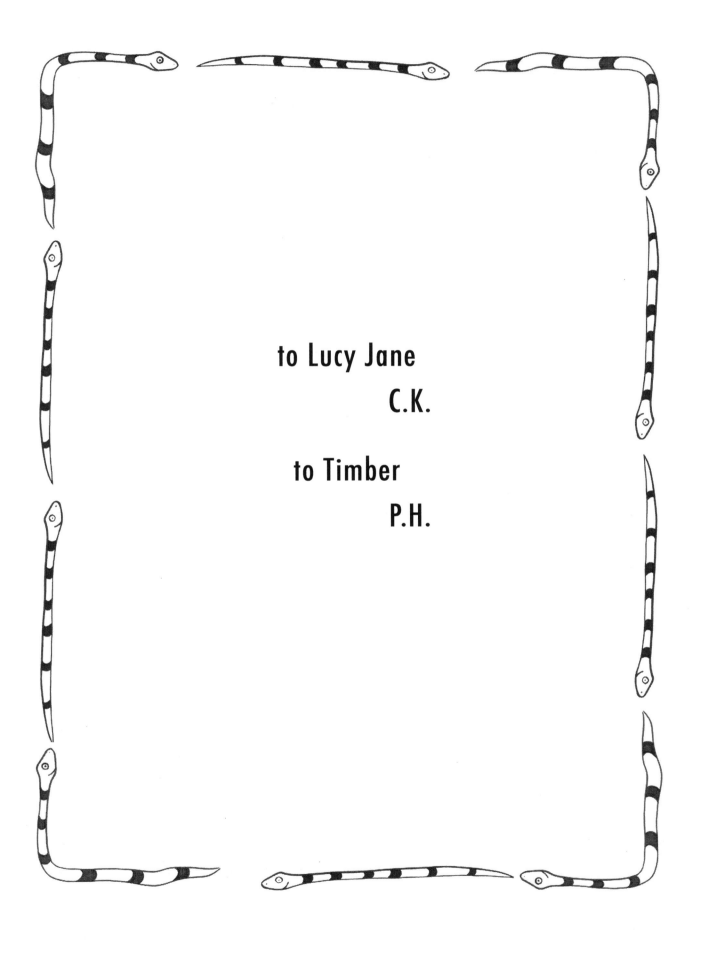

to Lucy Jane
C.K.

to Timber
P.H.

ALSO BY PAMELA HODGES

Color the Cats
How to Be a Cat

Hi!

This book belongs to:

_____

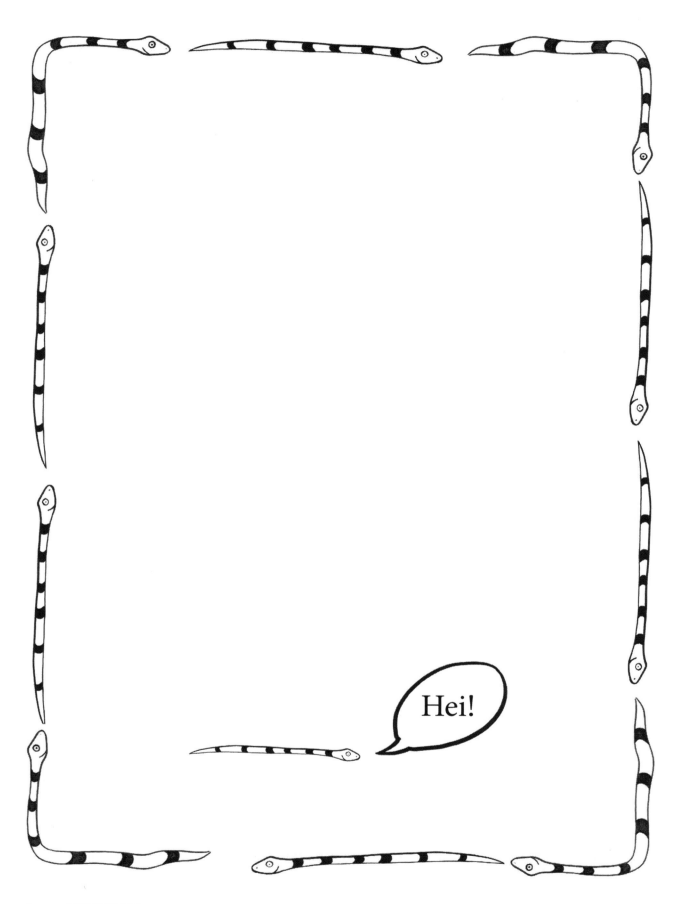

Table of contents

What you will need 11

PART ONE

Winden buys a guitar 15

PART TWO

Winden takes guitar lessons.....................................49

Lesson One: Parts of the guitar.............................51

Color the guitar 55

Lesson Two: Number the fingers.........................61

Lesson Three: Number the frets...........................65

Position markers 66

Lesson Four: Number the strings.........................69

Lesson Five: Name the strings 73

Let's tune your guitar 77

Open strings E, A, D, G, B, E 81

Alternate picking exercise 102

How to play a note 105

E note 107

F note 109

G note..112

3 note exercise...113

Table of contents

Reading music 115

Quarter note, half note 117

Whole note, rests 118

Staff, treble clef 119

Bar lines, time signature 120

Practice playing notes 121

Make up an exercise 141

Strumming 145

Chords 157

G chord 159

C chord 165

E minor chord.. 173

Strumming patterns 185

Dynamics.. 192

More notes 217

More chords 235

Fun songs to play 243

Author... 257

Squiggy 258

Illustrator 259

Extra sheet music and chord charts 260

What you'll need to play (learn) the guitar

1. A guitar:

Normally, a beginner will start out with an acoustic guitar of adequate size to their height. Make sure the guitar is not too big for the child. A three-quarter size guitar for a child is a good size to begin with.

2. A Tuner

It is important to play on a guitar that is in tune. You are training your ears to listen to the correct sound for each note on the strings of your guitar. You can purchase a small clip-on tuner or use tuning applications available for smart phones or to use on-line with a computer.

3. A guitar pick (Plectrum)

You don't have to have a pick to play the guitar. If you want to try using a pick, a light or ultralight pick is good for beginners as it is flexible.

4. A pencil

You don't need a pencil to play the guitar! But you will need a pencil for this book. This book is a workbook, with fill-in-the-blank pages for you to learn fingering, the parts of the guitar, numbering frets, the names of the strings, and music theory. You can even write your name in the book on page seven!

5. Crayons or markers (optional)

If you need a break from playing your guitar and want to flex other creative parts of your brain, there are many chances to color in this book.

Tansi!

Acoustic and electric guitars

The two main types of guitars are electric and acoustic. Both guitars have six strings, frets and use tuning pegs to tune the guitar.

An acoustic guitar has a large, hollow body with a sound hole beneath the neck of the guitar. An electric guitar has a thinner, solid body with no sound hole. An electric guitar uses electricity to send sound to a speaker.

Acoustic   **Electric**

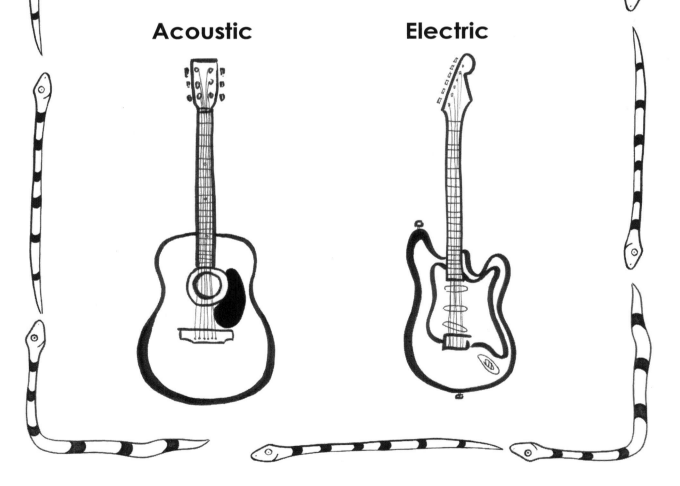

Color the pages with
your crayons
or colored pencils!
Have fun.

PART ONE

Winden buys a guitar

COREY KLAUS

Hi! I'm Winden, and this is my best friend, Squiggy.

I like to pretend I am a bear.

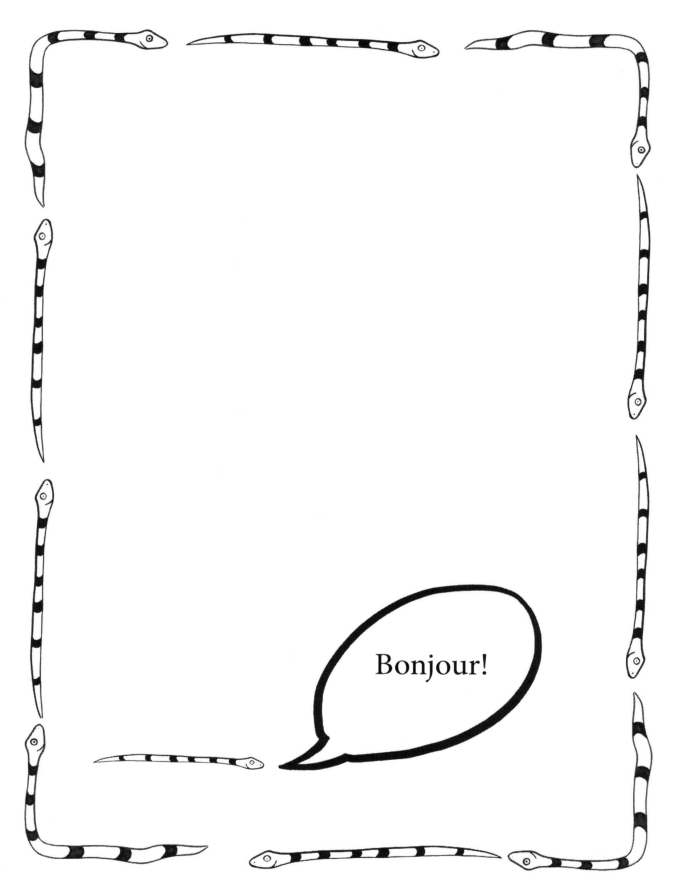

Sometimes, I pretend I am a tree.

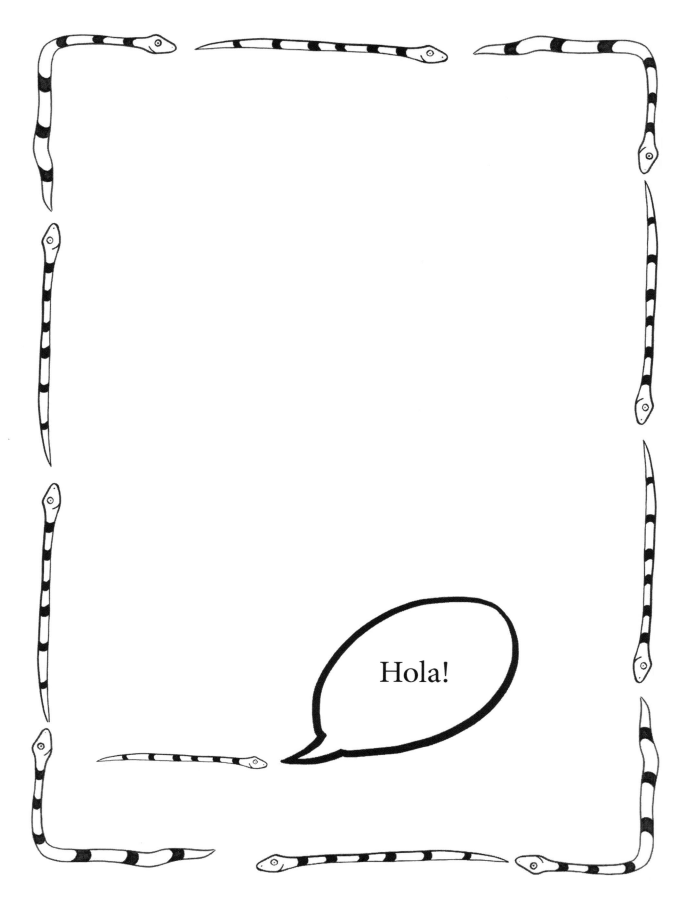

My favorite is pretending to be a rock star.

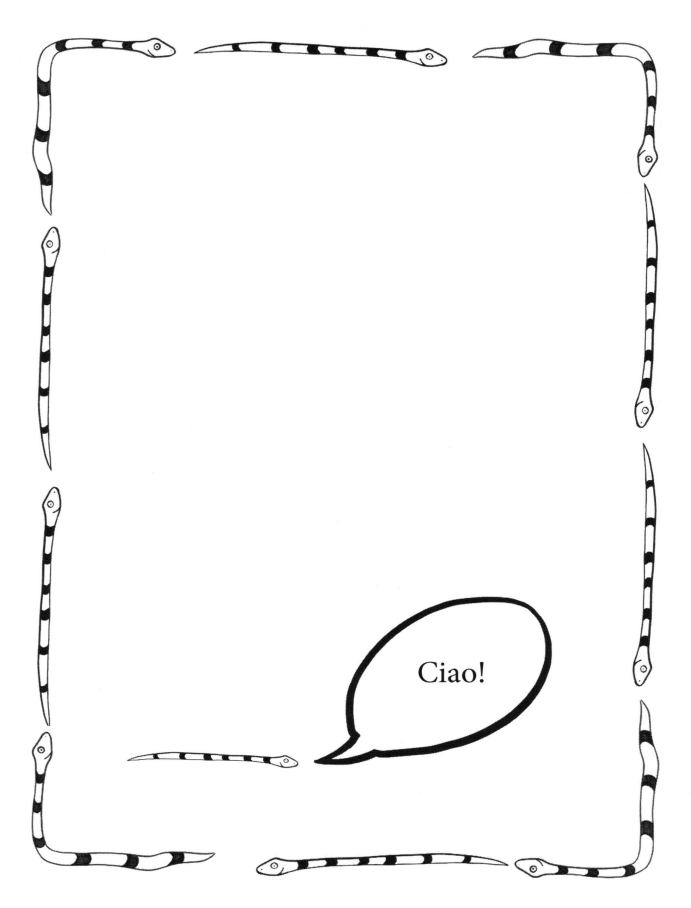

But first I need a guitar, not a broom!

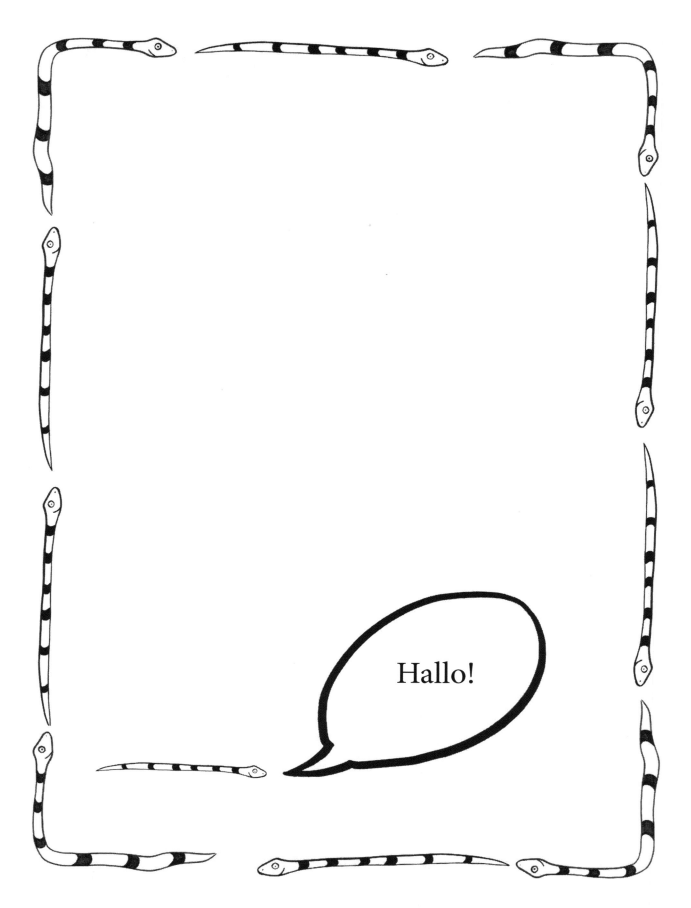

Will you help me pick out a guitar?

"Hi, I'm Winden. What's your name?"
"I'm Mr. Tom."

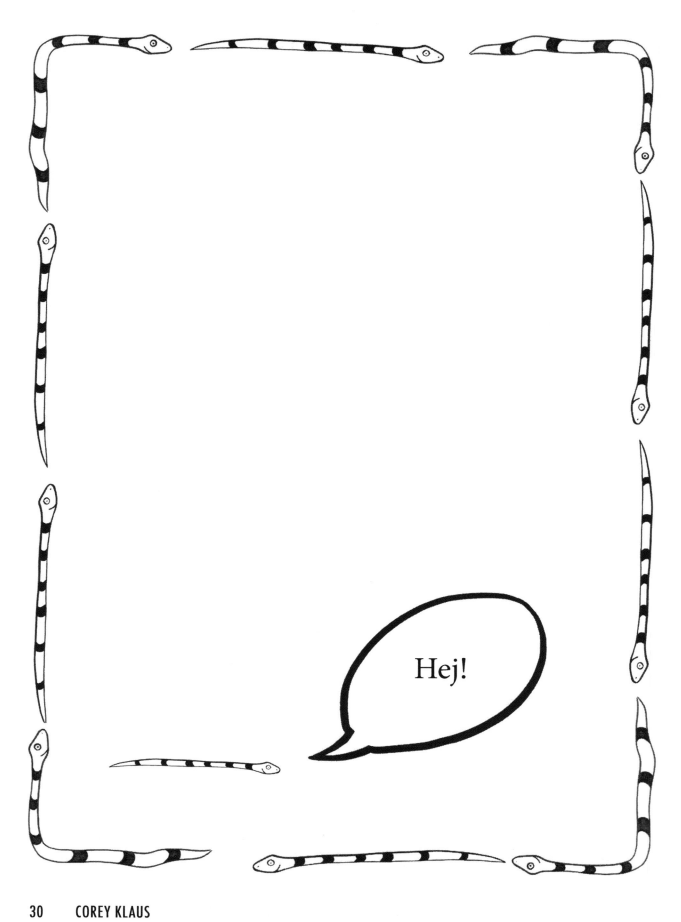

"Mr. Tom, what size guitar is right for me?"

COREY KLAUS

"Is this a good size, Mr. Tom?"

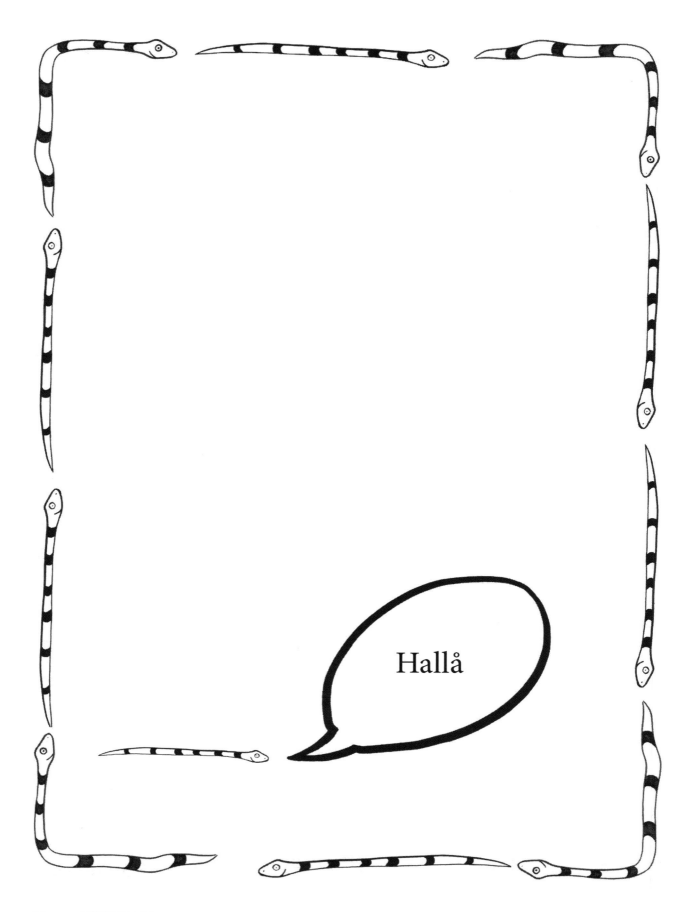

"No, it is too big for you."

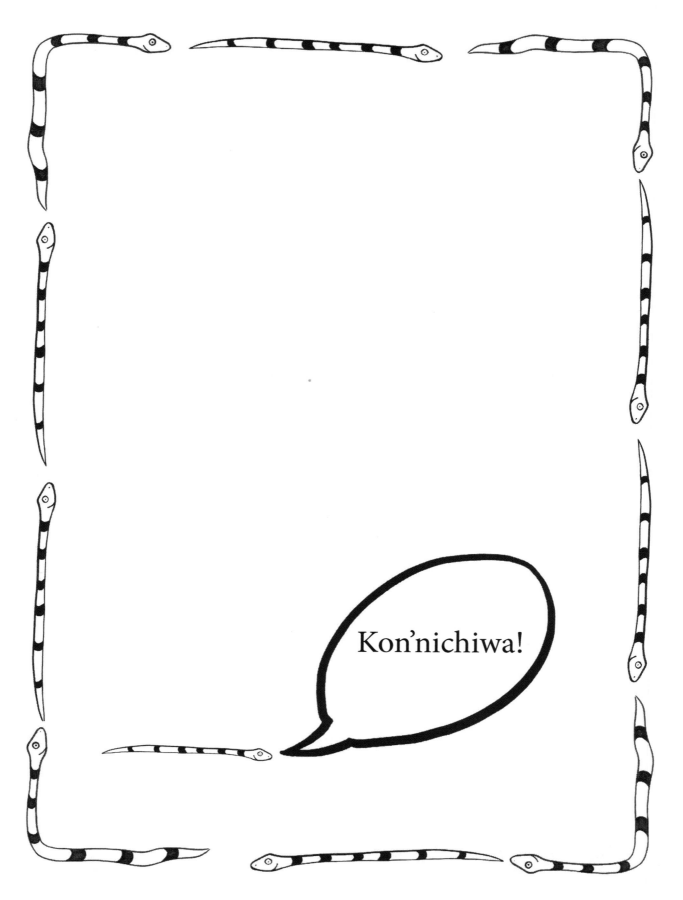

"What about this one?"

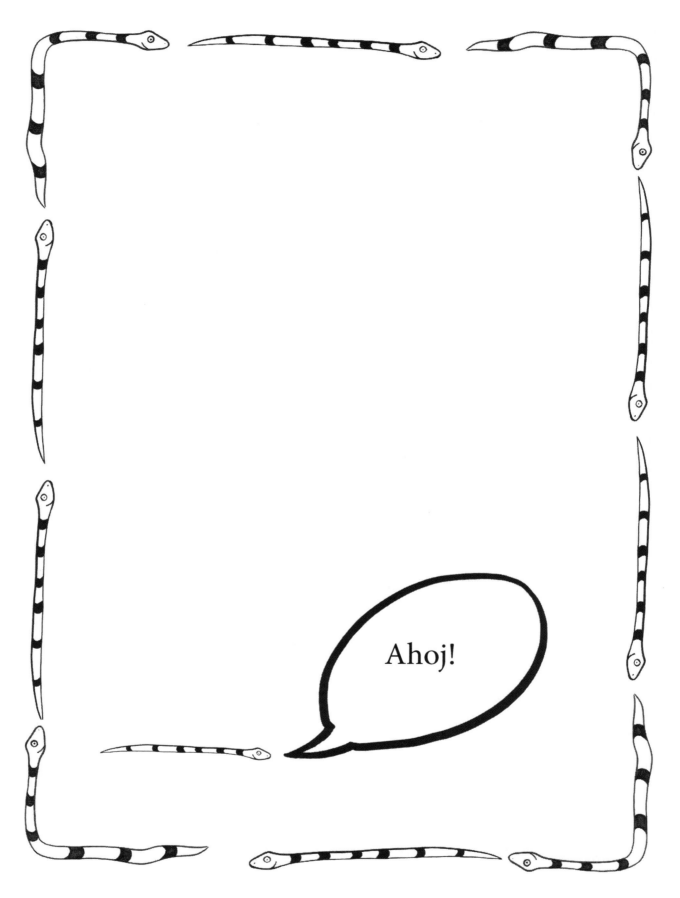

"One size guitar does not fit all.
Some are too big;
some are too small."

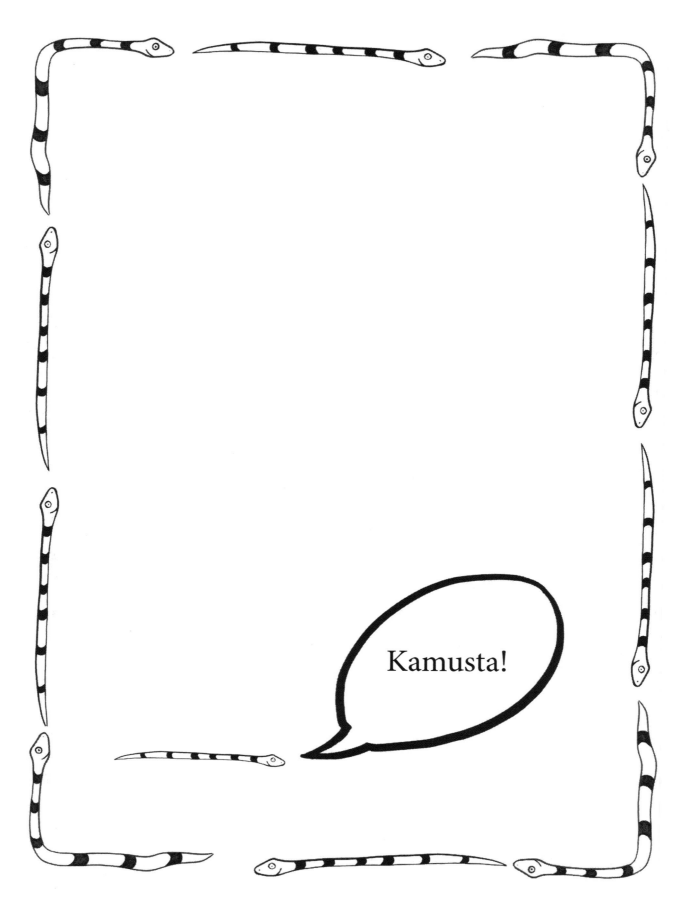

"Is this my size, Mr. Tom?"
"Yes, Winden. This one is your size."

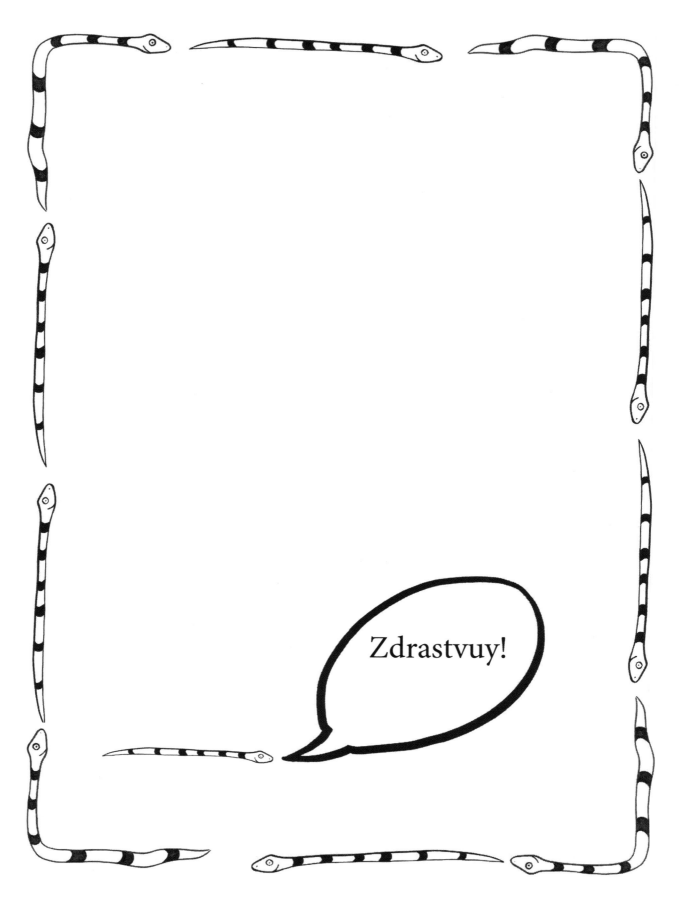

"Mr. Tom, how do I hold my guitar?" asked Winden.

"Put your left hand on the neck. Hug the guitar to your body, with the strings facing out," said Mr. Tom.

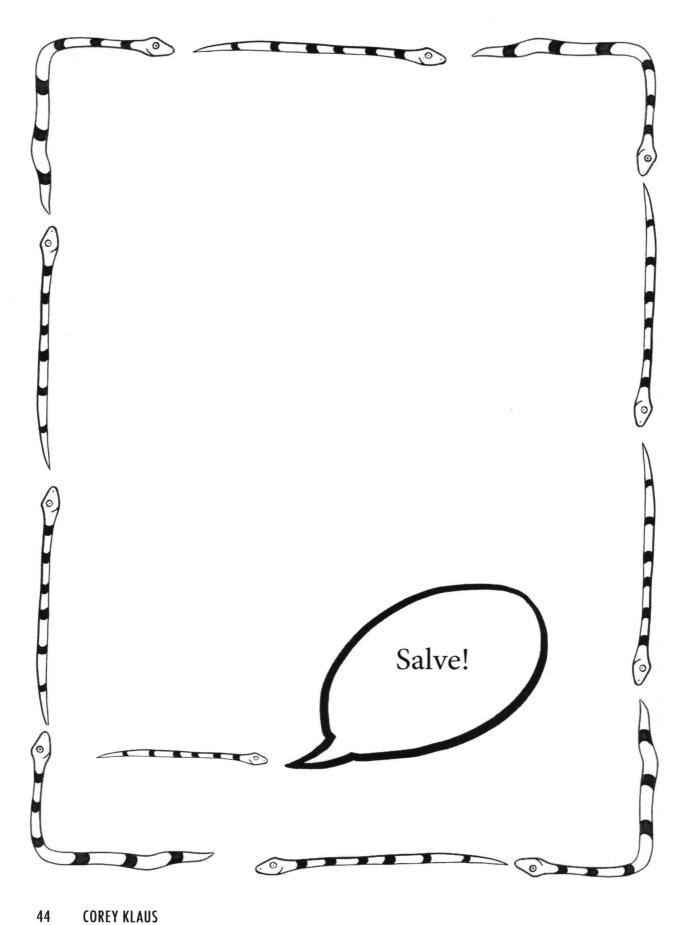

COREY KLAUS

Winden said, "I love it! This sounds great!"

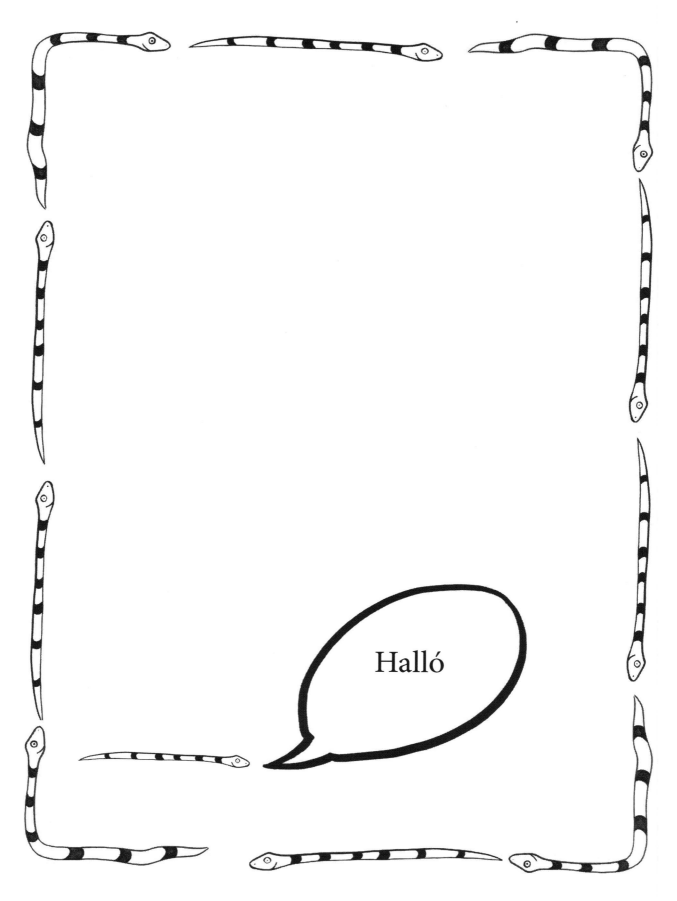

"Thank you for helping me pick out my guitar, Mr. Tom!"

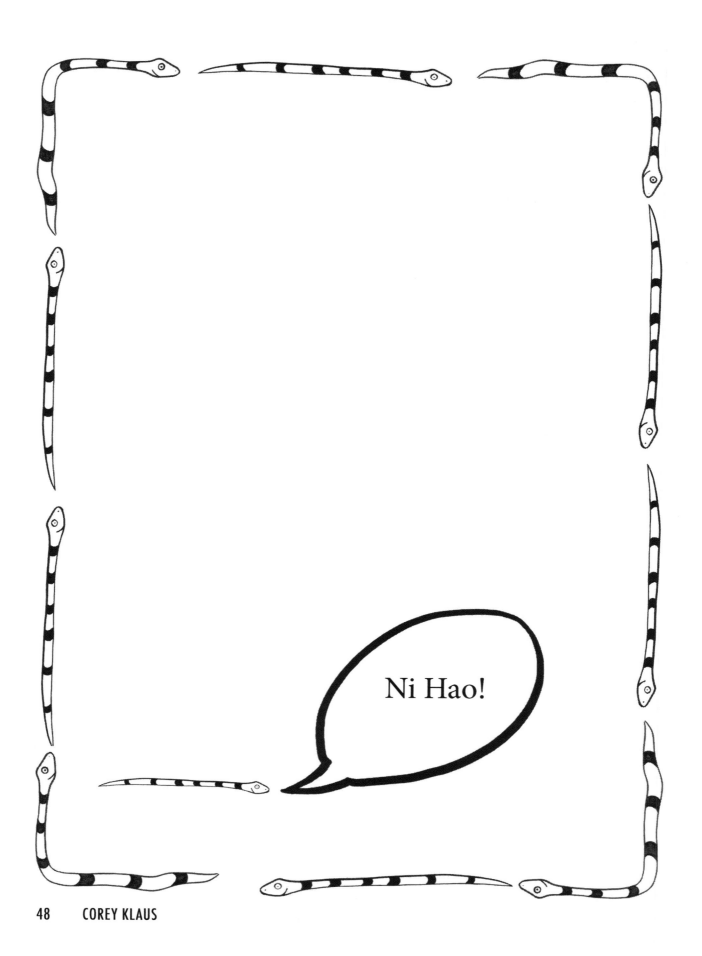

PART TWO

Winden takes guitar lessons

LESSON NUMBER 1
The parts of the guitar

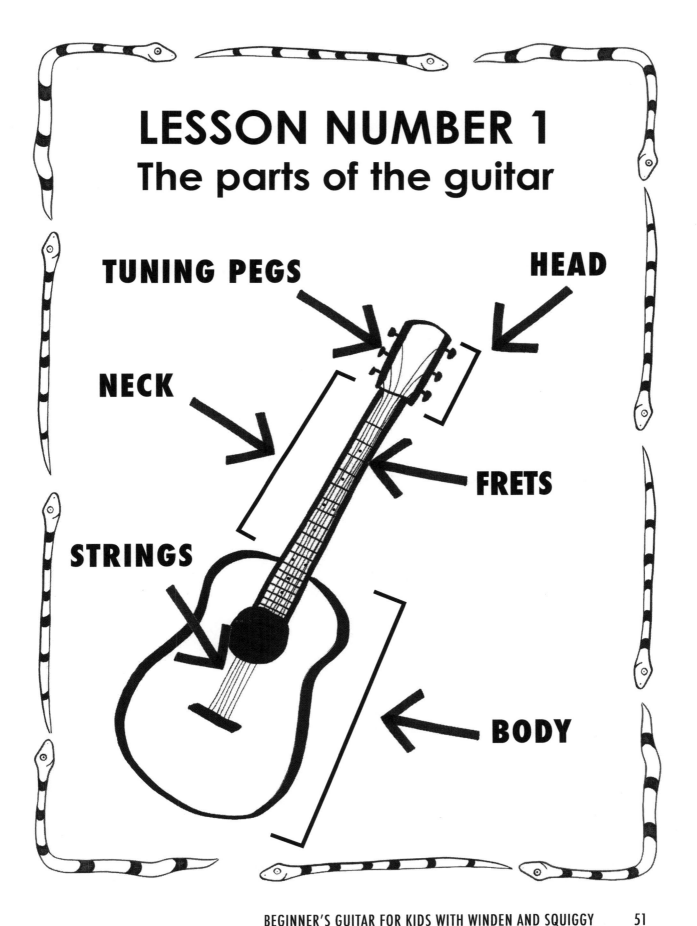

TUNING PEGS

HEAD

NECK

FRETS

STRINGS

BODY

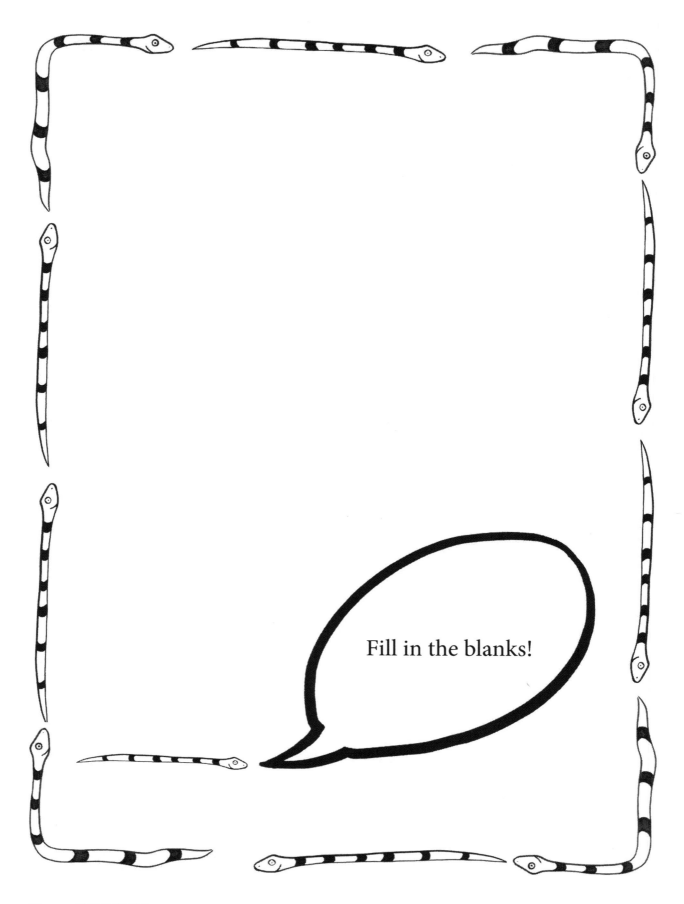

1: The parts of the guitar

Do you remember the parts of the guitar?
Fill in the blanks. It's okay if you look back.

Did you know a person who
makes or repairs guitars
is called a luthier?

COLOR THE GUITAR
DRAW A DESIGN!

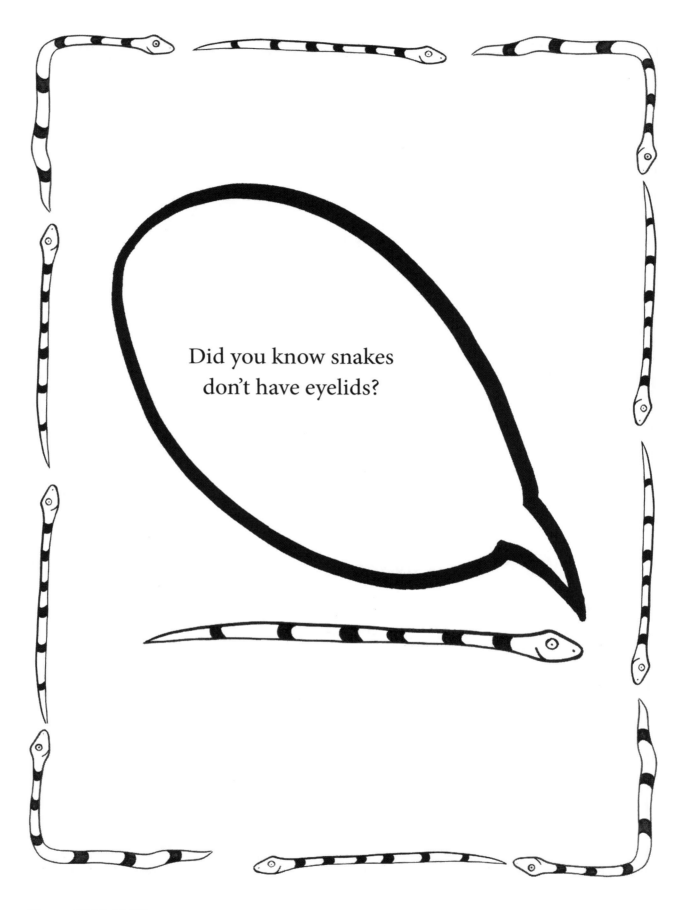

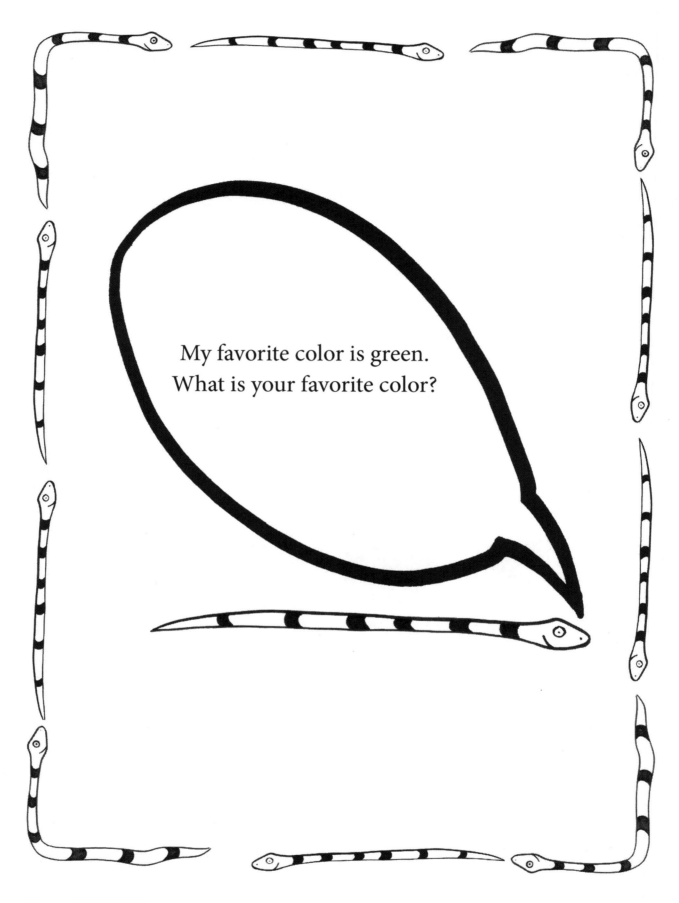

My favorite color is green.
What is your favorite color?

**COLOR THE GUITAR
DRAW A DESIGN!**

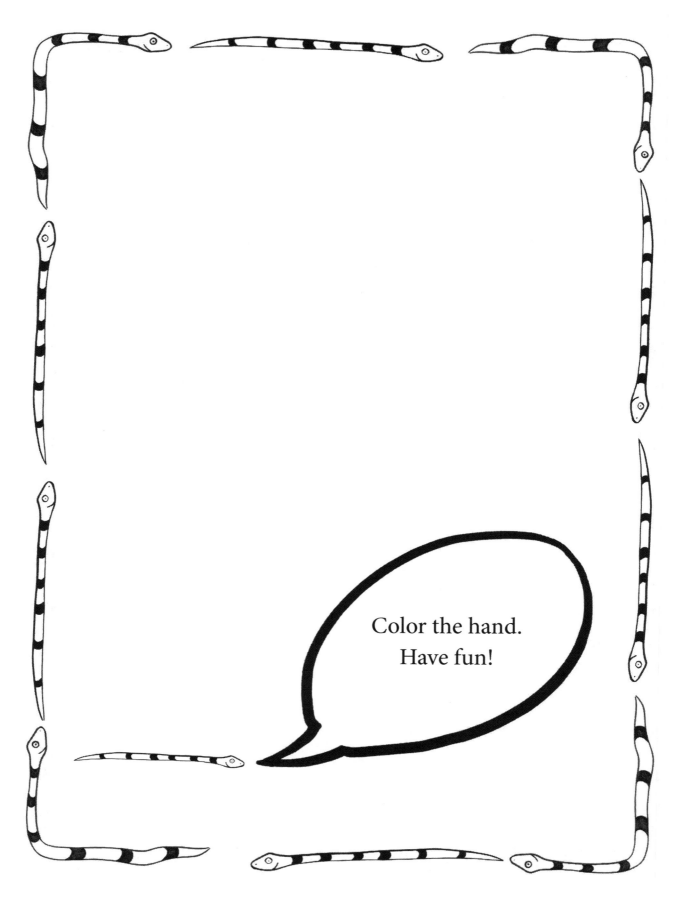

LESSON NUMBER 2
Number the fingers

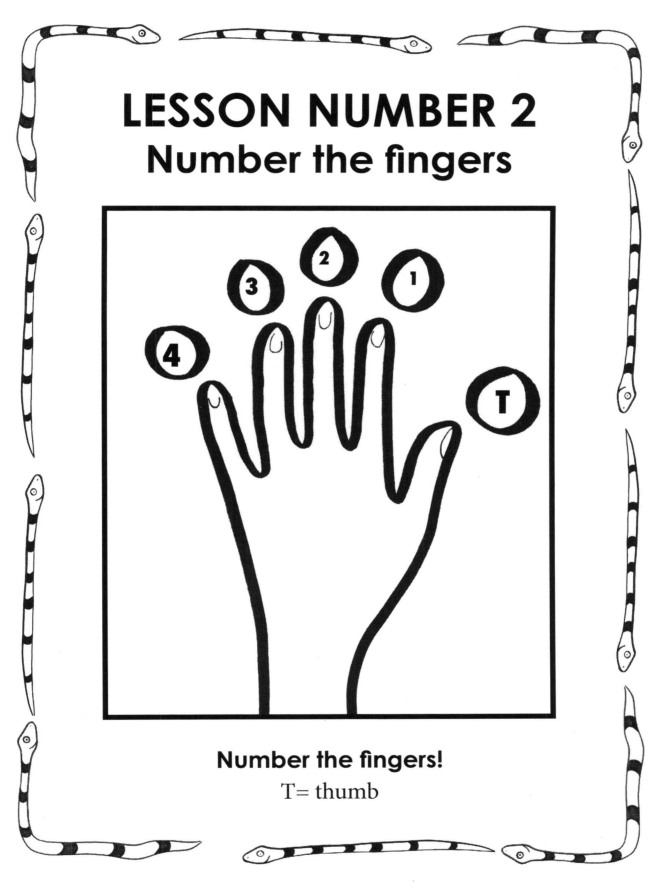

Number the fingers!
T= thumb

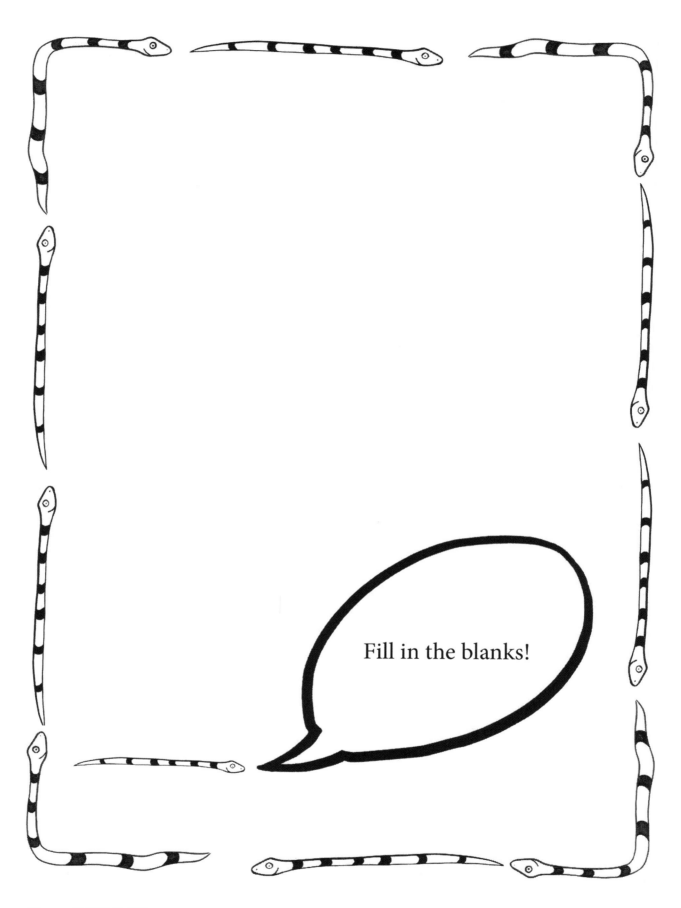

Fill in the blanks!

2: Number the fingers

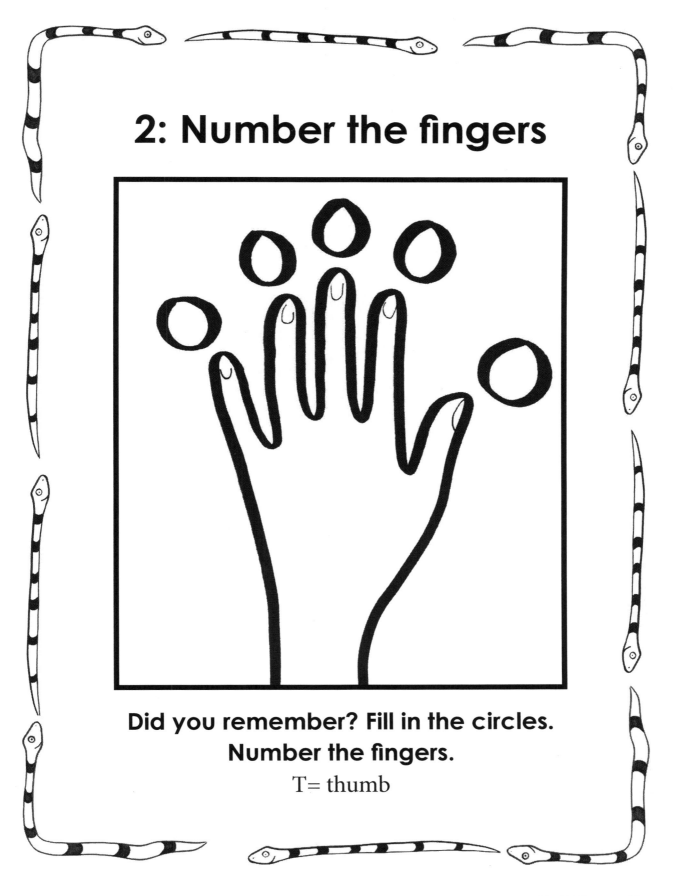

Did you remember? Fill in the circles.
Number the fingers.

T= thumb

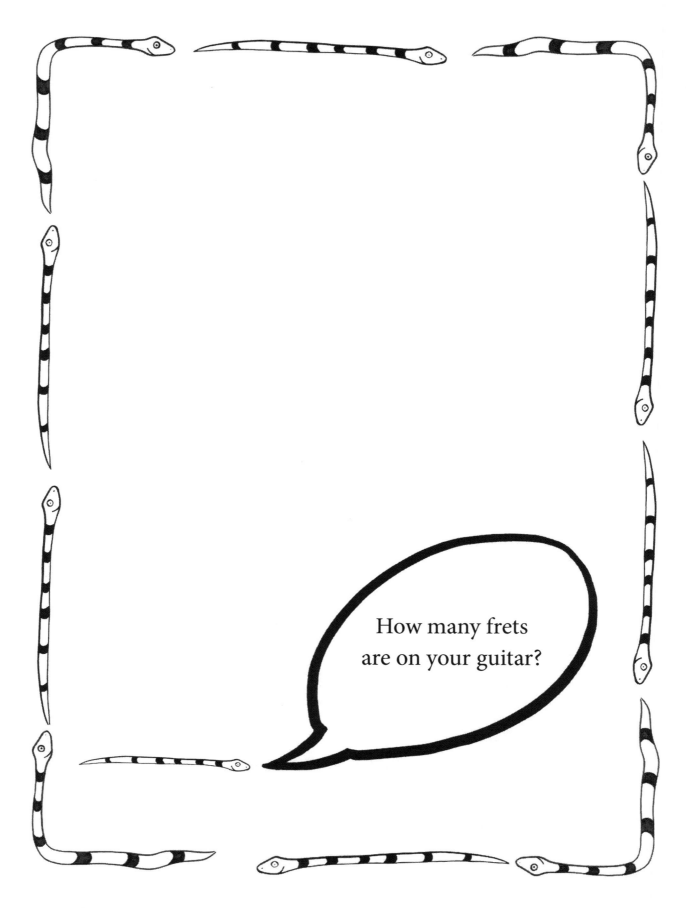

LESSON NUMBER 3
Number the frets

A fret is the thin piece of metal
on the neck of the guitar.

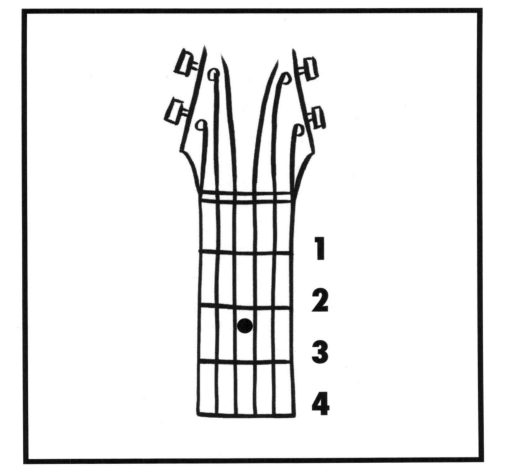

Number the frets.

(How many frets are on your guitar?
We only have the first four in this drawing.)

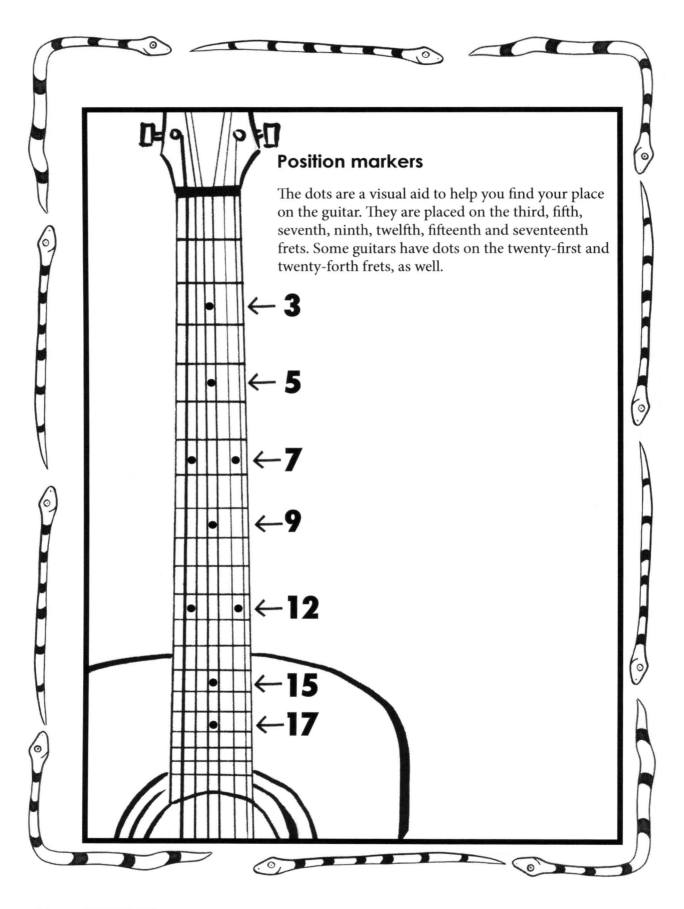

Position markers

The dots are a visual aid to help you find your place on the guitar. They are placed on the third, fifth, seventh, ninth, twelfth, fifteenth and seventeenth frets. Some guitars have dots on the twenty-first and twenty-forth frets, as well.

← **3**

← **5**

← **7**

← **9**

← **12**

← **15**

← **17**

3: Number the frets

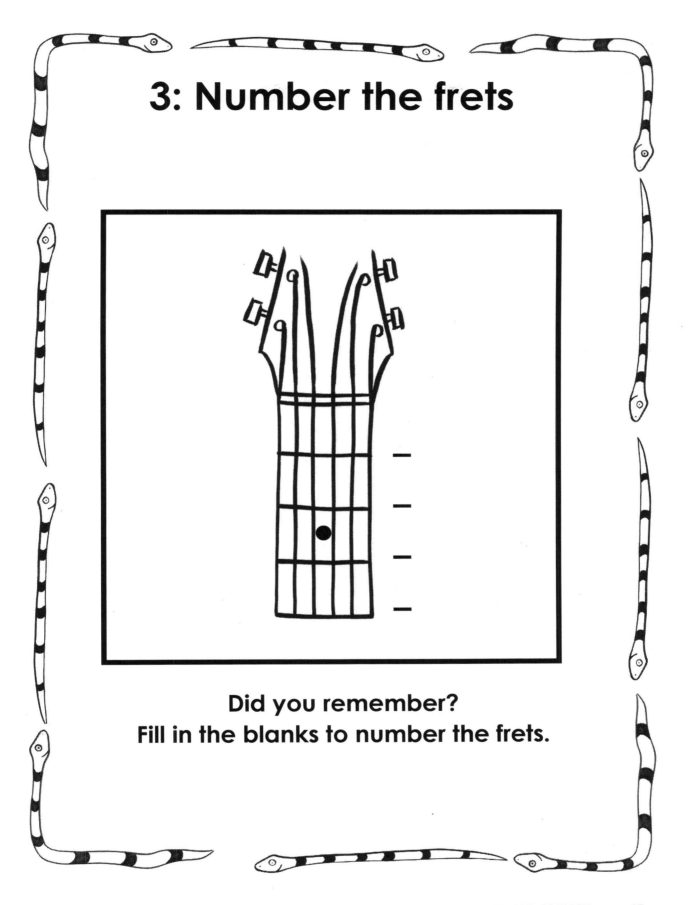

Did you remember?
Fill in the blanks to number the frets.

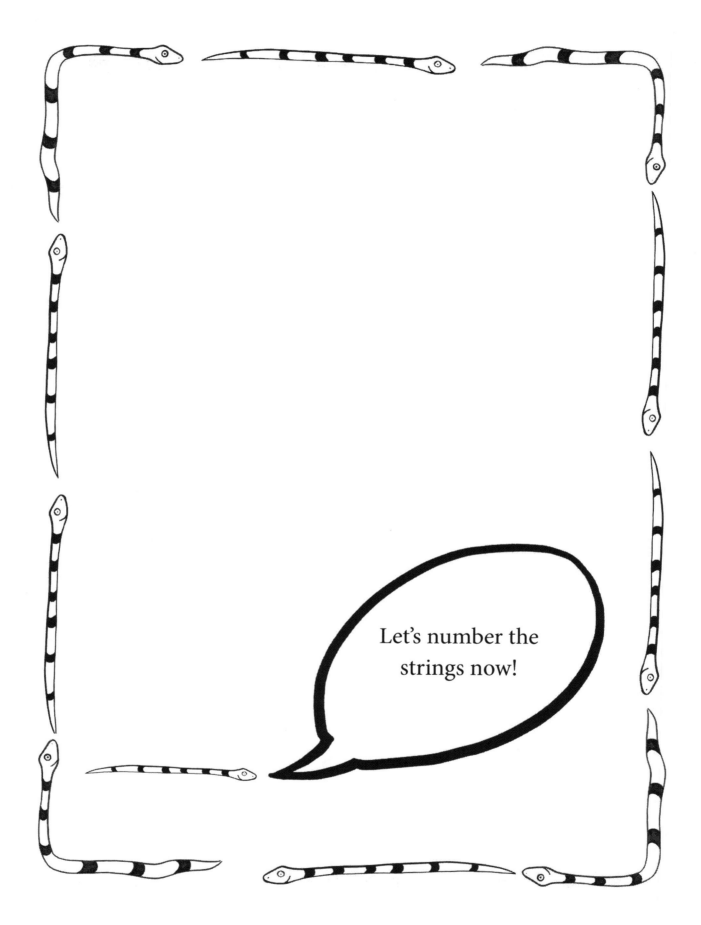

Let's number the strings now!

LESSON NUMBER 4
Number the strings

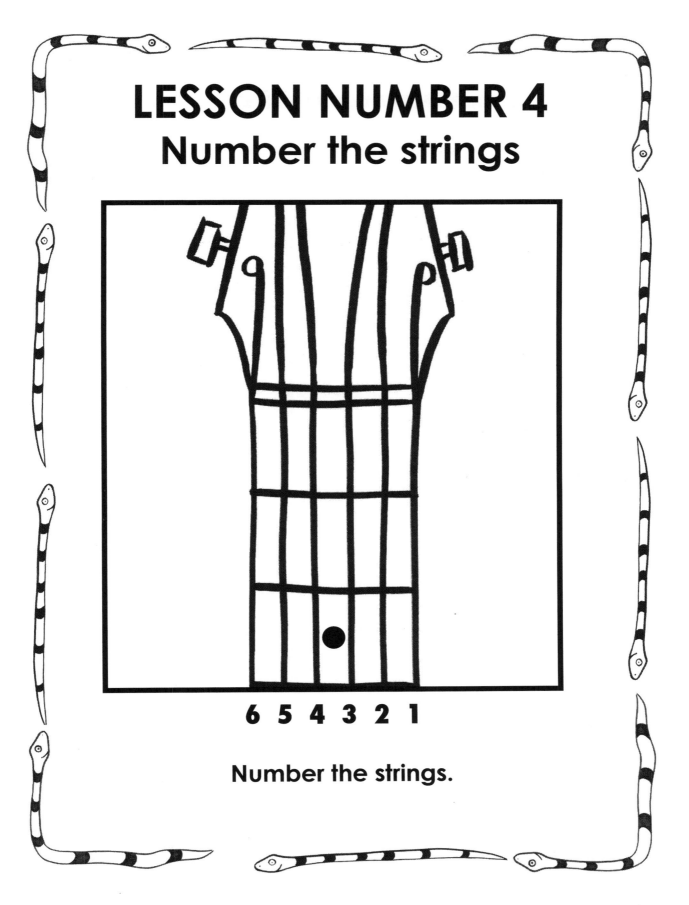

6 5 4 3 2 1

Number the strings.

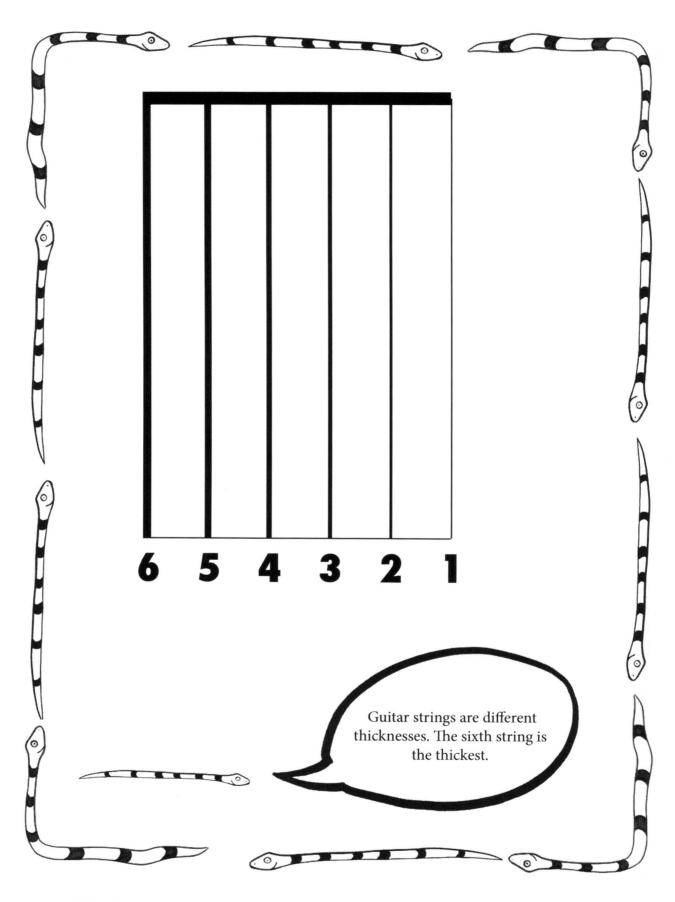

4: Number the strings

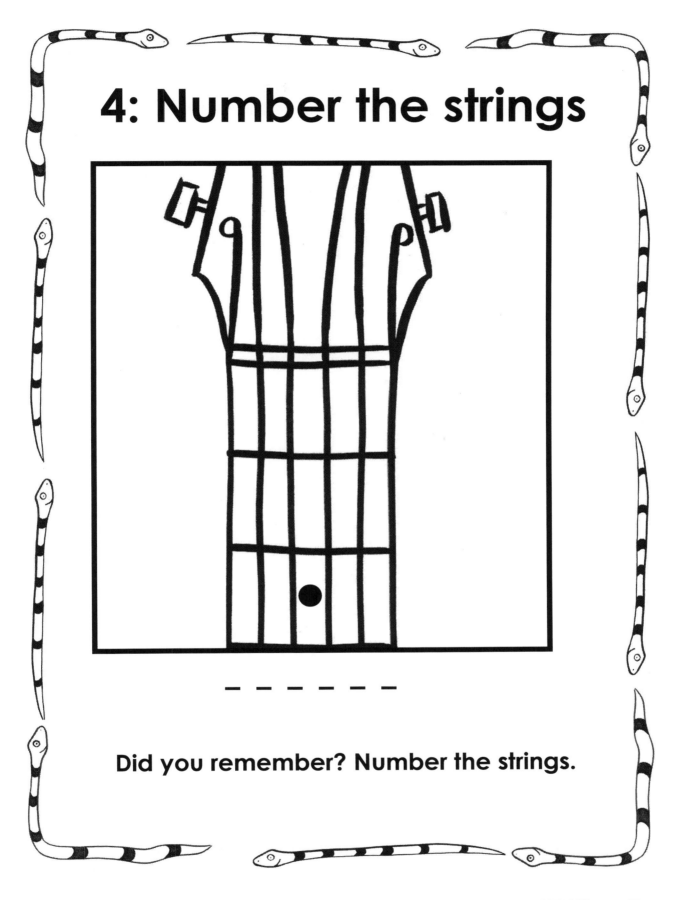

- - - - - - - -

Did you remember? Number the strings.

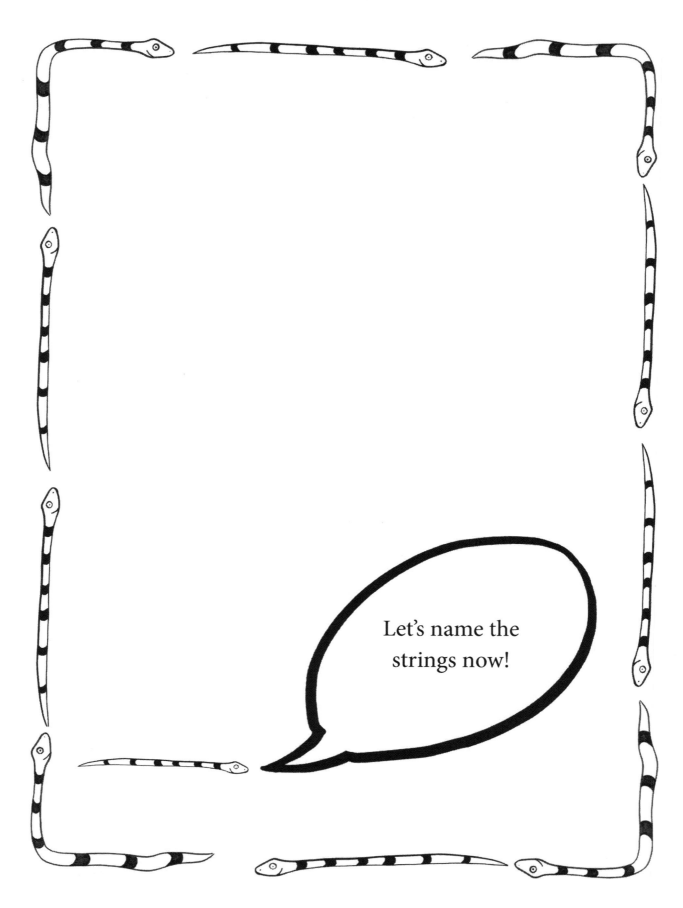

LESSON NUMBER 5
Name the strings

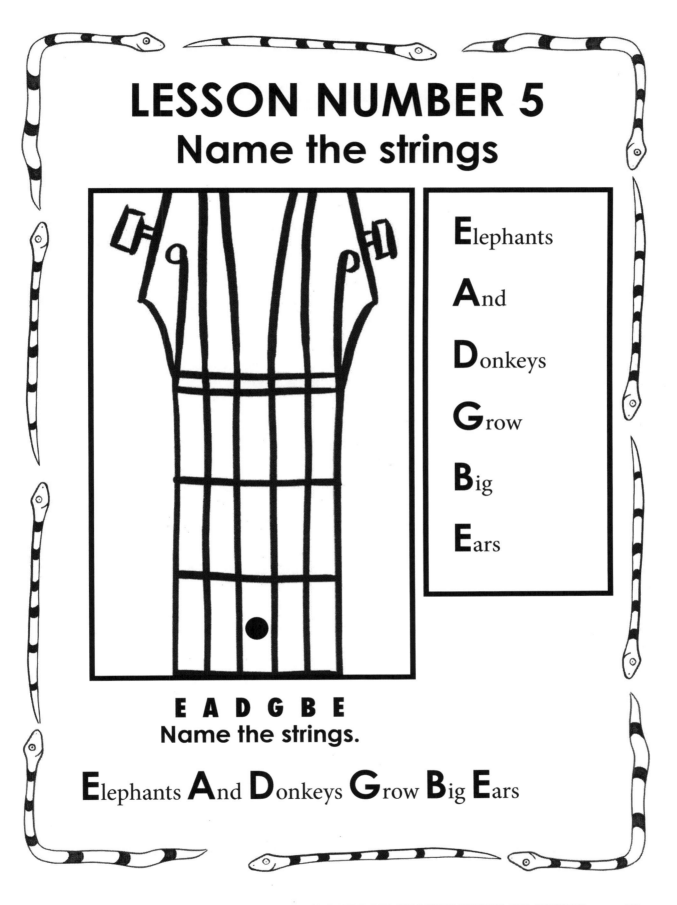

E l e p h a n t s

A n d

D o n k e y s

G r o w

B i g

E a r s

E A D G B E
Name the strings.

Elephants **A**nd **D**onkeys **G**row **B**ig **E**ars

5: Name the strings

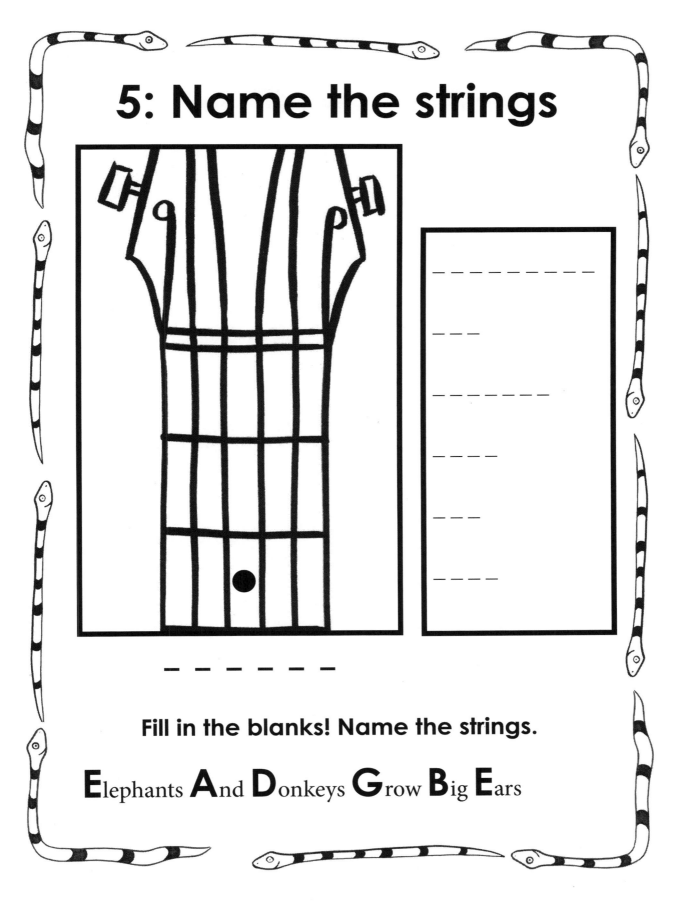

Fill in the blanks! Name the strings.

Elephants **A**nd **D**onkeys **G**row **B**ig **E**ars

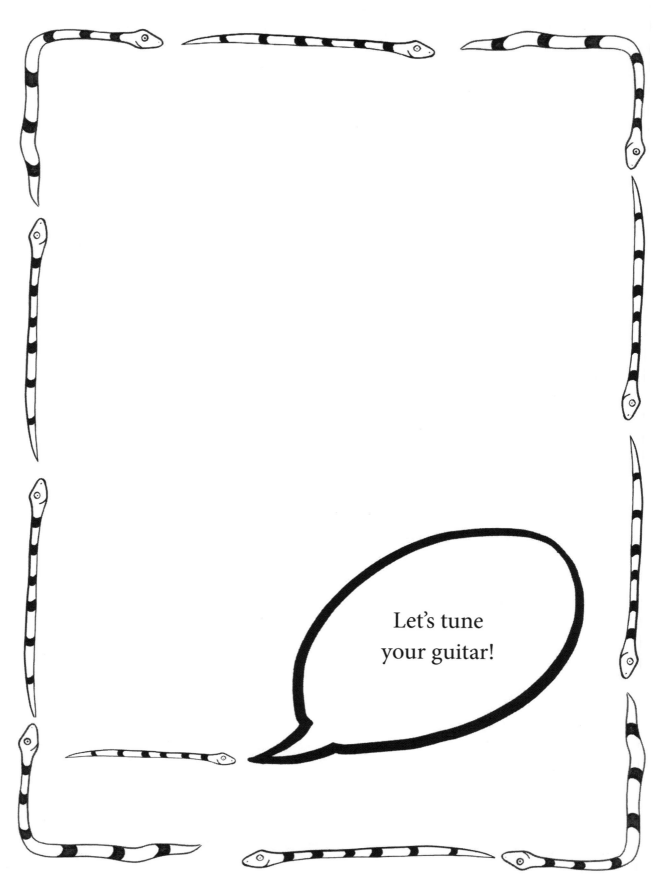

Let's tune
your guitar!

Before You Play
Let's tune your guitar!

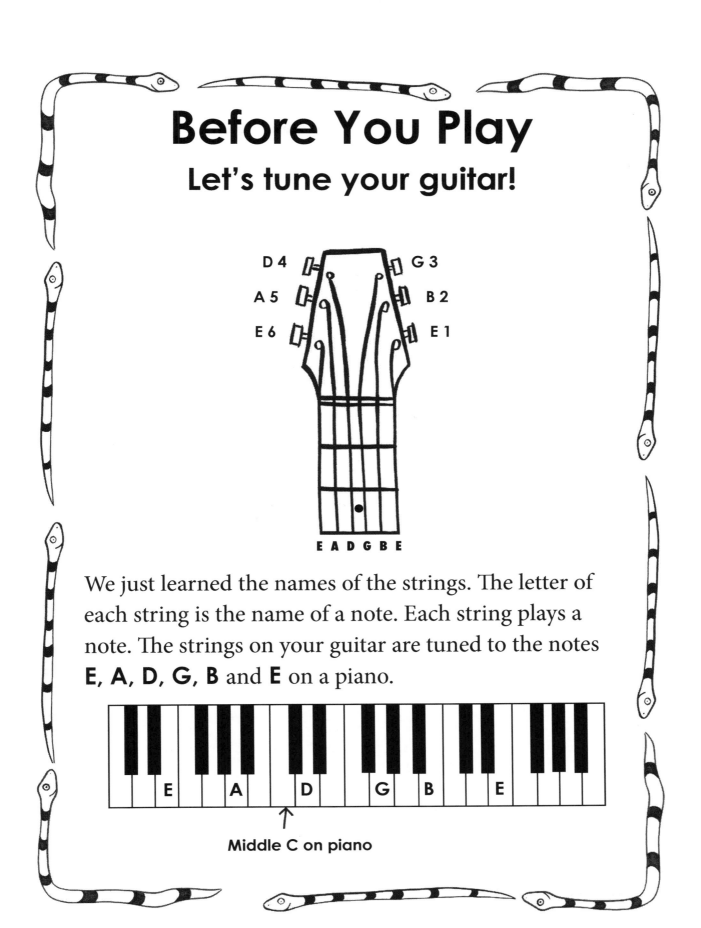

D 4   G 3
A 5   B 2
E 6   E 1

E A D G B E

We just learned the names of the strings. The letter of each string is the name of a note. Each string plays a note. The strings on your guitar are tuned to the notes **E, A, D, G, B** and **E** on a piano.

E   A   D   G   B   E

↑
Middle C on piano

Tune your guitar

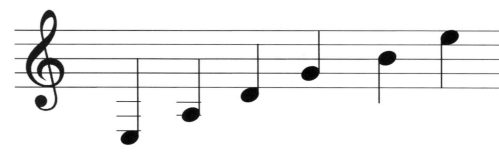

On the head of your guitar are the tuning pegs. Each peg is attached to one of the strings on the guitar. When you turn the tuning peg, it will make the note either higher or lower.

There are several ways to tune your guitar. You can use a piano to help you, or you can buy a small tuner that attaches to your guitar. There are also several tuning applications that are available for smart phones or to use online with a computer.

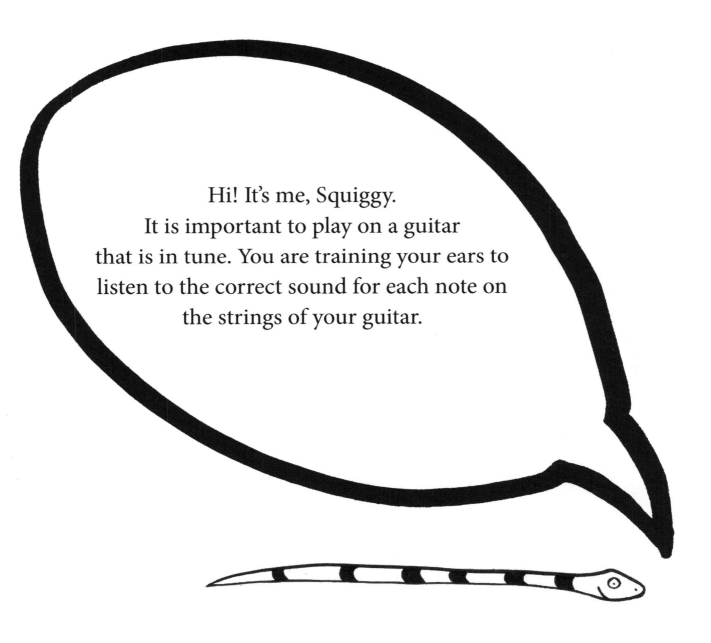

Hi! It's me, Squiggy.
It is important to play on a guitar
that is in tune. You are training your ears to
listen to the correct sound for each note on
the strings of your guitar.

Getting the feel for your guitar

Now that we introduced the names of the strings, let's play them and make some noise!

Open strings

When we play a string without pressing down on the string with our left hand on the neck, it is called an "open" string. Just remember: Open hand - Open strings.

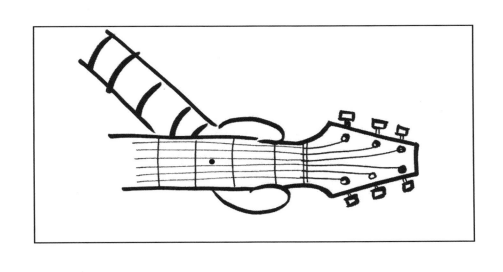

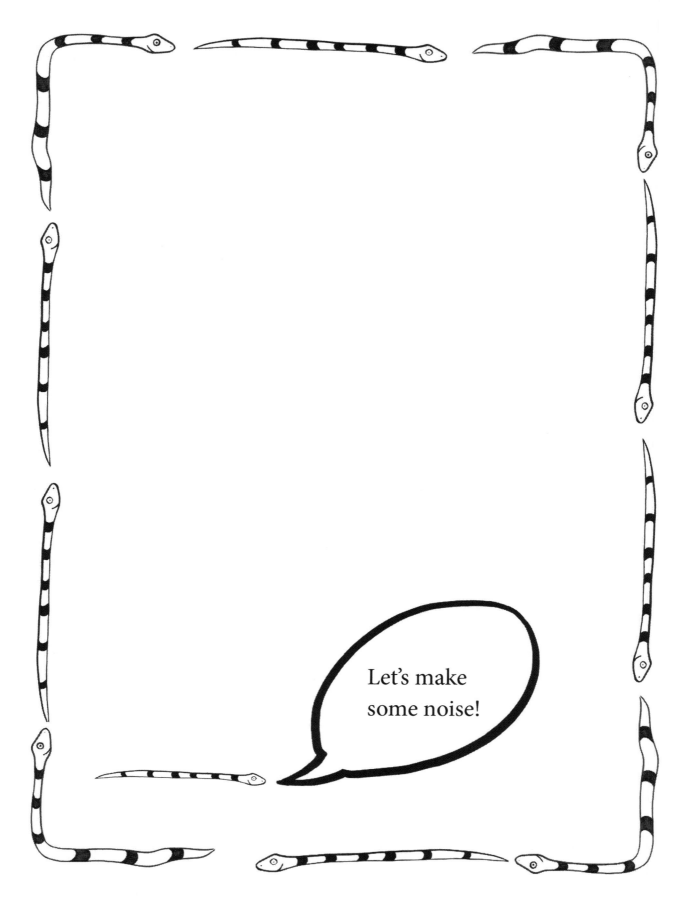

If you have trouble remembering or matching the right strings to the ones on the page, just hold your guitar up to the drawing of the guitar neck on this page. Or cut out one of the drawings from the back of the book that shows the names of the strings.

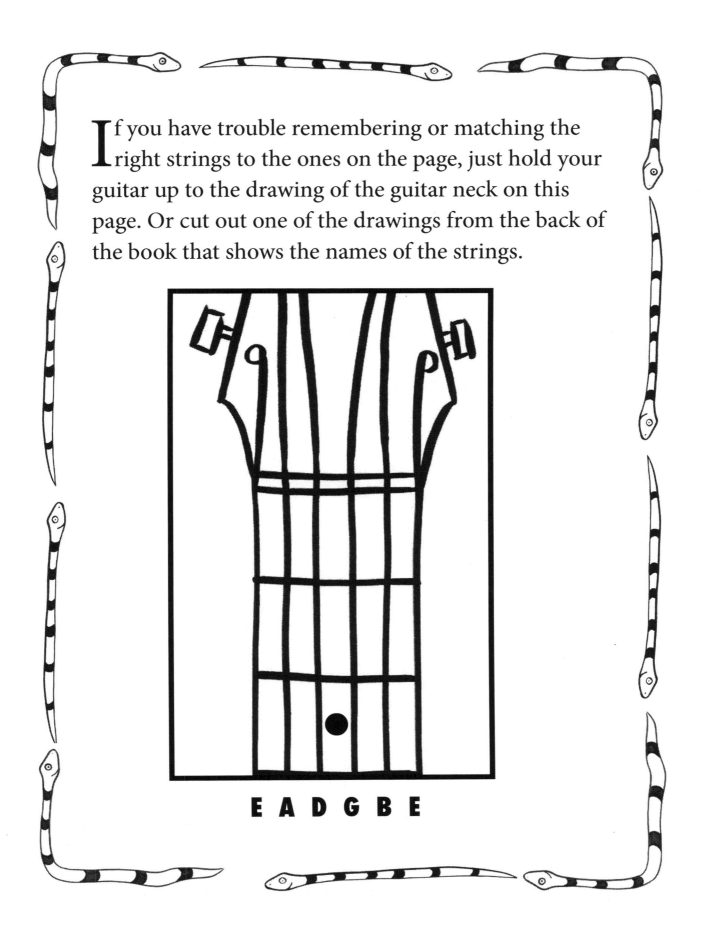

E A D G B E

The back of the guitar

Keep your thumb in the middle of the back of the guitar, behind the second fret.

You are doing a great job!

How to hold a guitar

Sit in a chair that has no arms. You want to be able to move your hand freely without hitting the arm of the chair.

Place the curve of the bottom of the guitar on top of your leg. Hold the guitar tight to your body. Hold the neck of the guitar with your left hand. Place your thumb behind behind the second fret on the neck of the guitar.

How to hold a pick

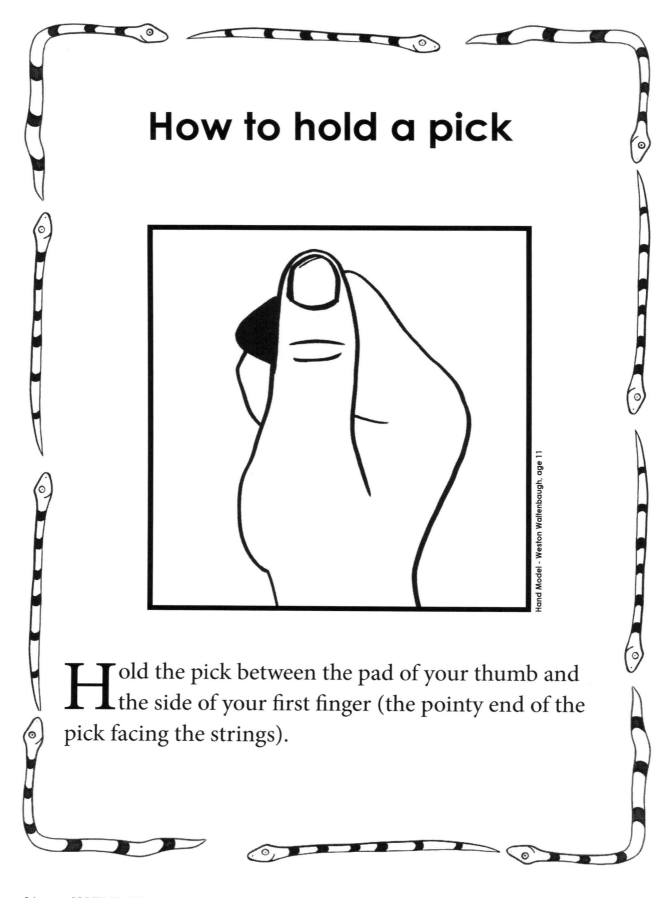

Hand Model - Weston Waltenbaugh, age 11

Hold the pick between the pad of your thumb and the side of your first finger (the pointy end of the pick facing the strings).

We are going to play each string, one at a time.

If you have a pick, hold it with the hand you will use to play the strings. Hold the pick between the pad of your thumb and the side of your first finger (the pointy end of the pick facing the strings). If you don't have a pick to use, use your fingers/thumb to pluck or glide across each string.

Start at the top with your sixth (E) string (the thick one), and pick that string, keeping your left hand away from touching the strings on the neck as you play each individual string.

Play the string over the sound hole and experiment. Call out the name of the string while you play it. Eeeeeeee! Aaaaaaaa! Ddddddd! Gggggggg! Bbbbbbbbb! Eeeeeeeeee!

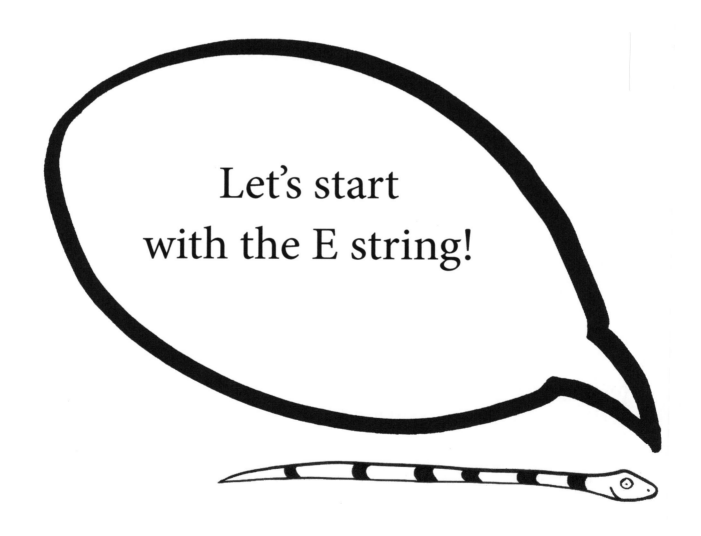

Elephants

And

Donkeys

Grow

Big

Ears

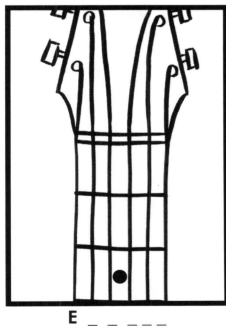

E _ _ _ _ _

Play the E string.

Hello!

COREY KLAUS

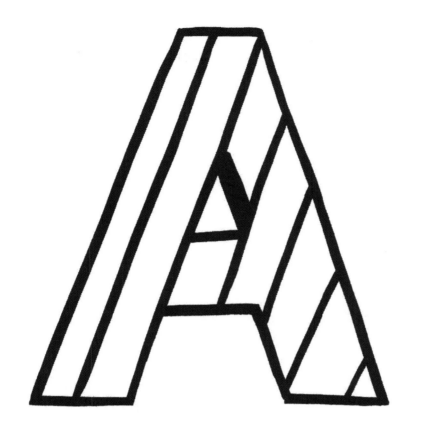

Elephants

And

Donkeys

Grow

Big

Ears

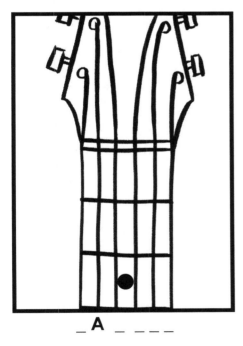

_ A _ _ _ _

Play the A string.

COREY KLAUS

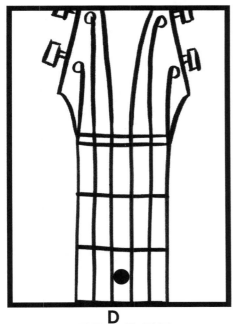

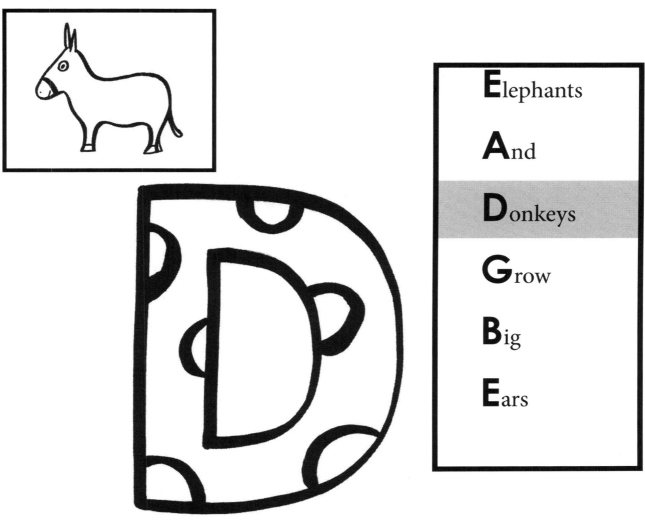

Elephants	
And	
Donkeys	
Grow	
Big	
Ears	

Play the D string.

_ _ D _ _ _

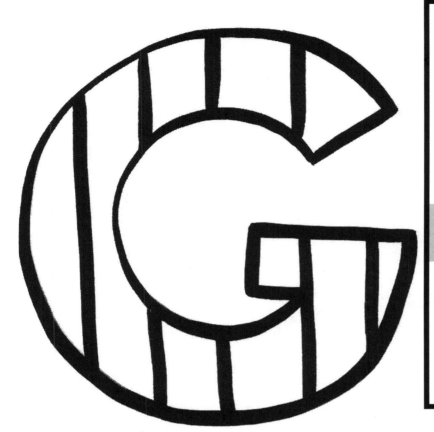

Elephants

And

Donkeys

Grow

Big

Ears

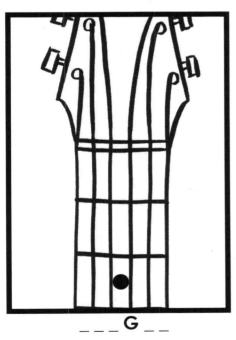

_ _ _ G _ _

Play the G string.

B is for big! The anaconda is the largest snake in the world.

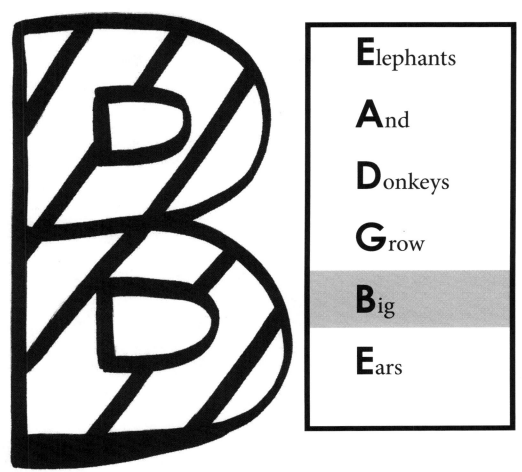

Elephants

And

Donkeys

Grow

Big

Ears

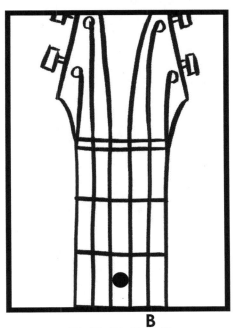

_ _ _ _ **B** _

Play the B string.

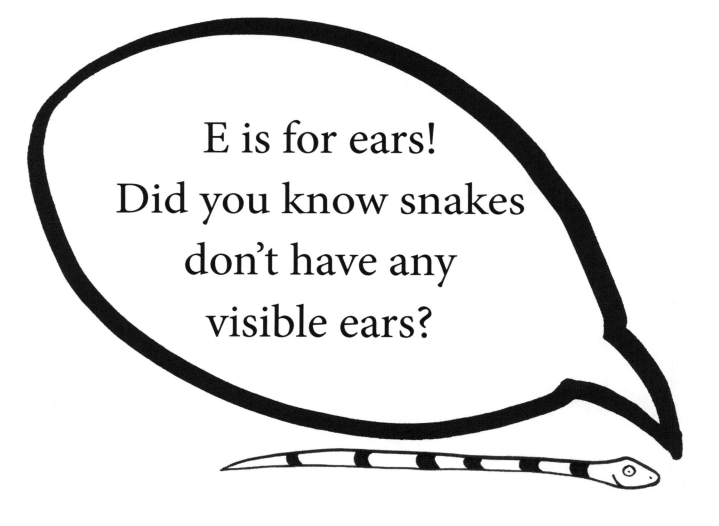

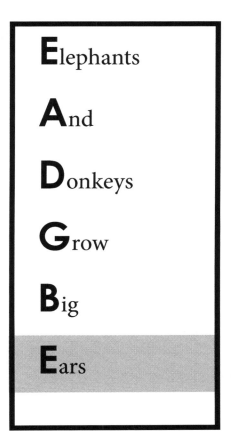

Elephants

And

Donkeys

Grow

Big

Ears

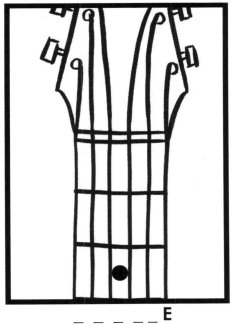

E

Play the E string, the first string.

E A D G B E

Practice Playing the Strings

E A D G B E

Can you remember the names of the strings?

Let's practice!

Call out the names of the strings as you play.

Alternate picking exercise

This exercise focuses on the picking aspect of playing guitar. You can do this exercise with open strings or by holding a chord. (We will learn chords on page 157.)

With your right hand, while holding your pick, strike the top sixth (E) string four times, E E E E, picking down - up - down - up.

You will do this for all six strings from top to bottom and then bottom to top. Hinging from the elbow, your wrist must be kept straight. Start slow and gradually increase speed as you become more comfortable.

It's better to be slow and accurate than fast and sloppy.

∏ = Down Pick
V = Up Pick

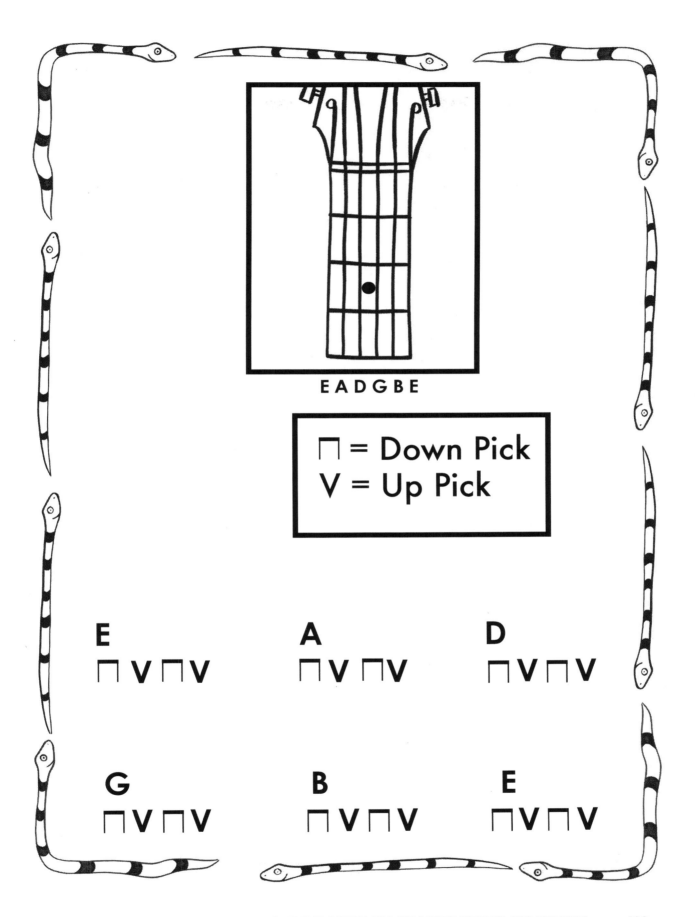

EADGBE

☐ = Down Pick
V = Up Pick

E
☐V☐V

A
☐V☐V

D
☐V☐V

G
☐V☐V

B
☐V☐V

E
☐V☐V

How to play a note

We are going to learn how to play three notes:

E, F and G.

The notes E, F and G
are on the same string, the first (E) string.

With one hand behind the neck of the guitar, use your
other hand, or thumb, to play the strings. You pick a
string to play a note.

Go fast or slow.
Let the notes ring out for as long as you'd like.
Be creative and don't forget: Have fun!

The back of the guitar

Rember to keep your thumb in the middle of the back of the guitar, behind the second fret.

I believe in you!

E note:

First string

Next, play the first string Open, without any fingers holding down any strings on the frets; this is called the E open.

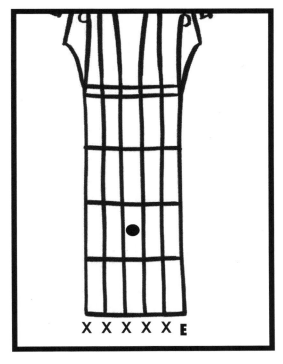

X X X X X E

Pick the first string (E) of your guitar. Make sure you are not muting the strings with your left hand on the neck. Keep your thumb behind the second fret.

F note

First string, first fret, first finger

Put your first finger on the first fret of the first string; this is the F note.

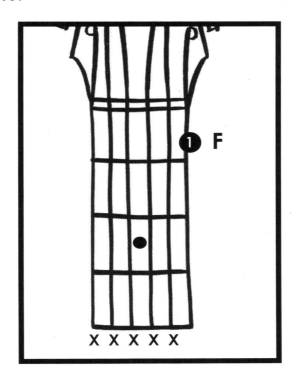

x x x x x

Pick the first string (E). This time, place your 1st finger behind the 1st fret on the string as shown. Keep the thumb of your left hand behind the 2nd fret to anchor yourself to one spot.

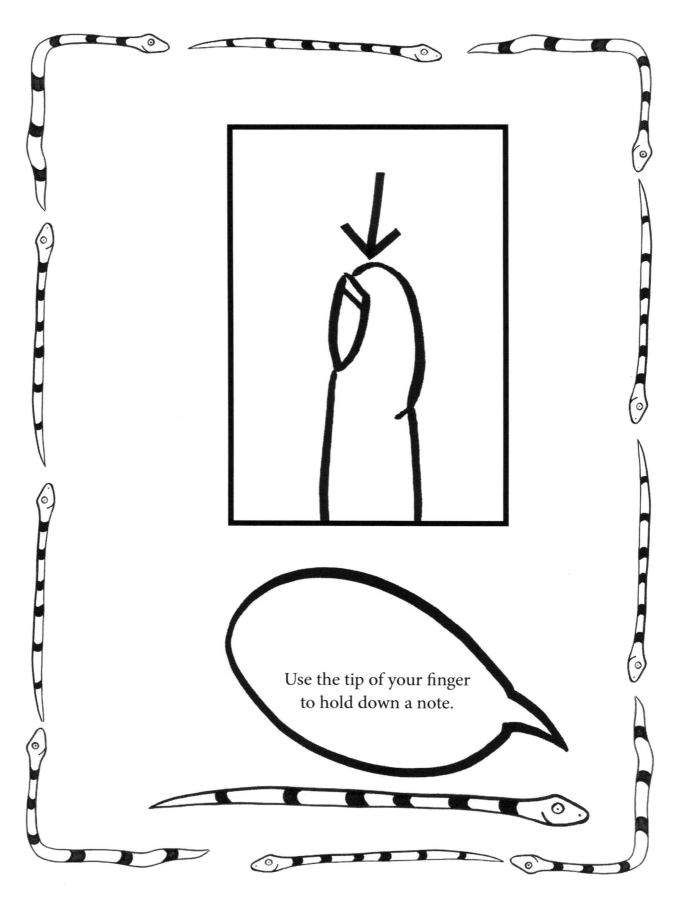

Use the tip of your finger
to hold down a note.

F note: first fret, first string

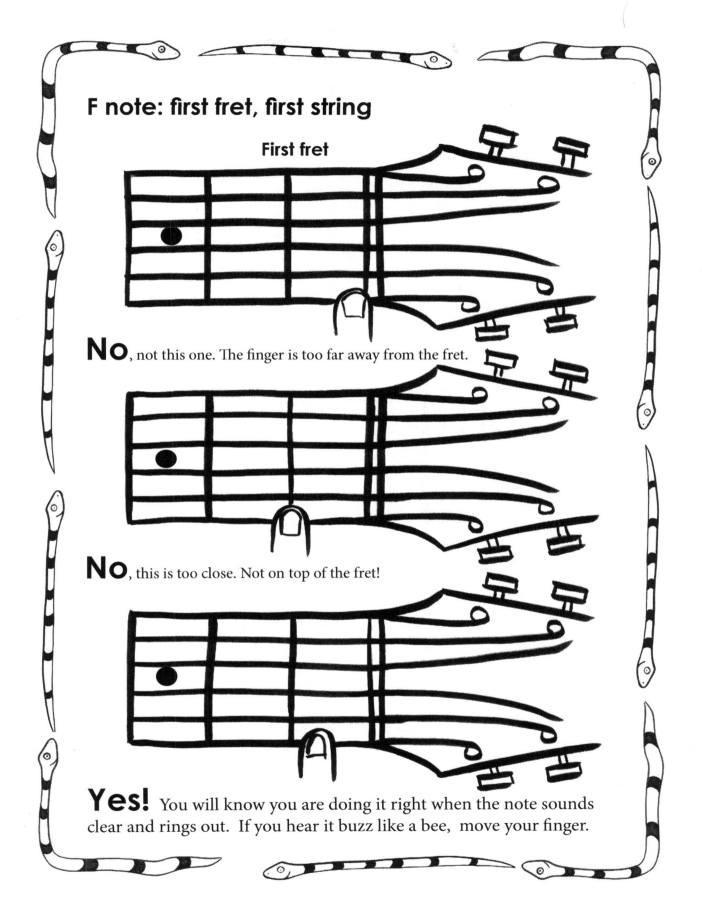

First fret

No, not this one. The finger is too far away from the fret.

No, this is too close. Not on top of the fret!

Yes! You will know you are doing it right when the note sounds clear and rings out. If you hear it buzz like a bee, move your finger.

G note:

First string, third fret, third finger

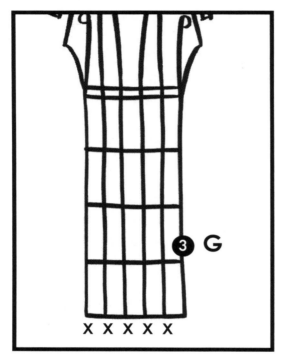

W hile keeping your thumb behind the second fret, stretch your third finger to the third fret on the first string. Using your right hand, gently pick the same string that you are holding down with the other hand, ideally over the sound hole of your guitar.

This is the G note.
And now go the other way.
Play E open, and then the F with the first finger on the first fret, and feel the stretch all the way to the third fret. Try it out and see!

3 note exercise:

Instead of learning how to read music right now, I want you to focus on the notes you are playing. These exercises will contain the letter of each note and how many times to play it.

In the exercises shown, play each note for every syllable to each word.

```
E  E  E   E      E   E
E  is for el - e - phant
```

```
F  F  F   F
F  is for frog
```

```
G G G   G G  G G
G is for go-rill-a foot
```

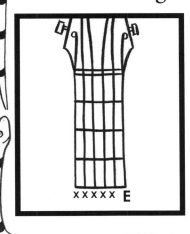 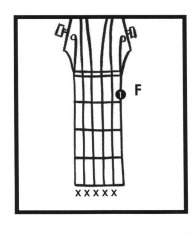 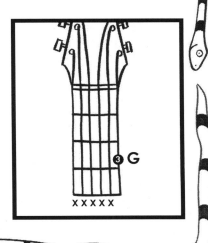

3 note exercise:

Front to Back and Back to Front!

In this exercise you will play E-F-G and then play those same notes in reverse.
This is a good way to learn notes and finger dexterity; it is also a great finger warm-up before playing.

Ready? Go!

Front to back E-F-G
Back to front G-F-E

Back to front G-F-E
Front to back E-F-G

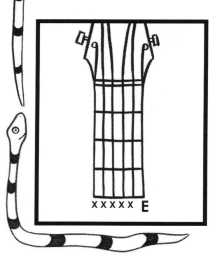 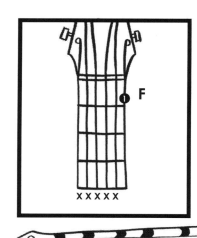 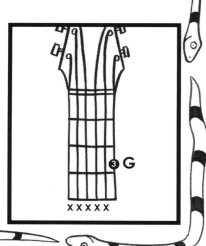

Reading music

Let's learn how
to read music now.

Notes:

Some notes are held for longer than others.

Quarter note

When a note is black with a stem, it is called a quarter note. A quarter note is held for 1 beat. Just play it and count to one.

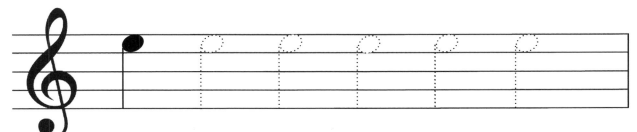

Draw a quarter note. Remember to fill in the circle.

Half note

When you see an open circle, not colored in, with a stem, it is a half note. A half note is held for two beats. Just play it and count to two.

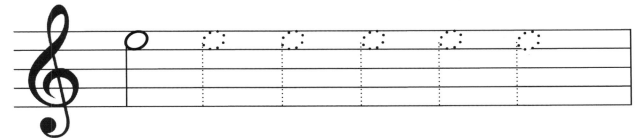

Draw a half note. This time we don't fill in the circle

Whole note

A whole note looks like an open circle, not colored in, with no stem. A whole note receives four beats. Just play it and count to four.

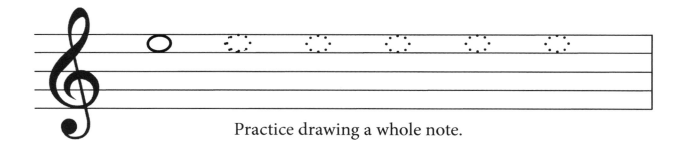

Practice drawing a whole note.

Rests

A rest means you don't play a note. You count silently.

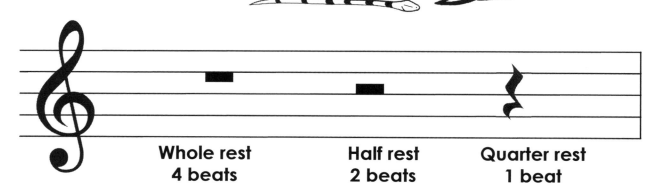

Whole rest	Half rest	Quarter rest
4 beats	2 beats	1 beat

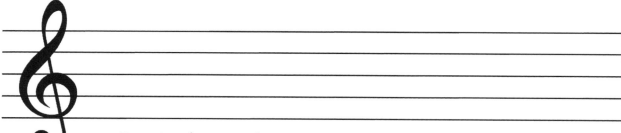

Practice drawing the rests.

Staff

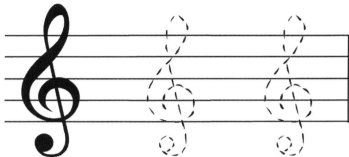

Music is written on a staff. There are five lines and four spaces.

Treble Clef

Guitar music is written in the treble clef.

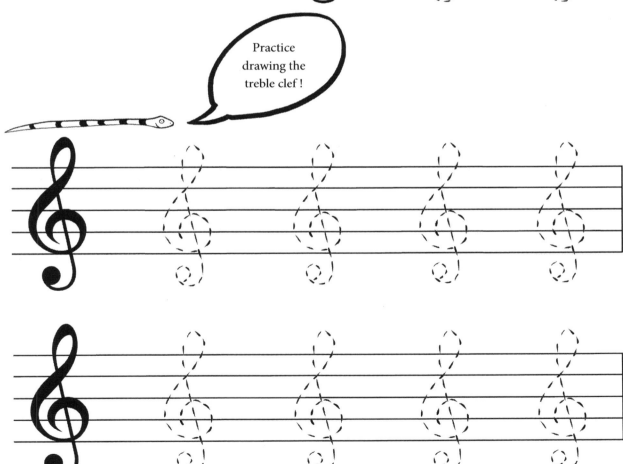

Practice drawing the treble clef!

Bar lines

The bar lines divide up the staff. A **measure** is the section on a musical staff between two bar lines. A **double bar** at the end of a staff is the end of the piece of music.

Measure

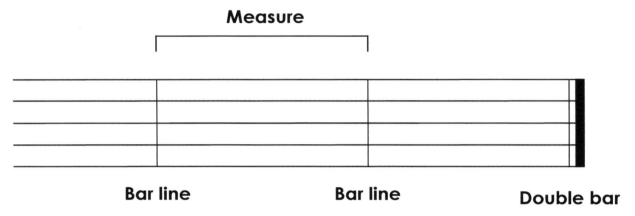

Bar line   **Bar line**   **Double bar**

Time Signature

The time signature is next to the Treble Clef.

The number on top tells you how many beats are in one measure. This time signature has four beats in one measure

The number on the bottom of a time signature tells you the type of note that will get one beat.

Four beats in one measure: a quarter note gets 1 beat

E note

Let's practice playing the E note. You don't have to hold down the string with a finger on a fret. Let's practice counting. There are 4 beats in one measure.

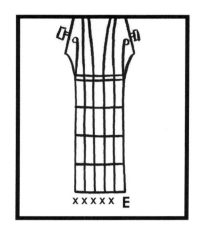

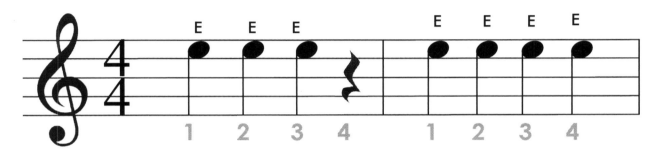

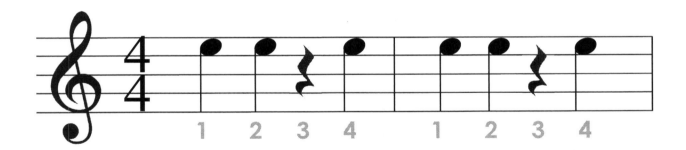

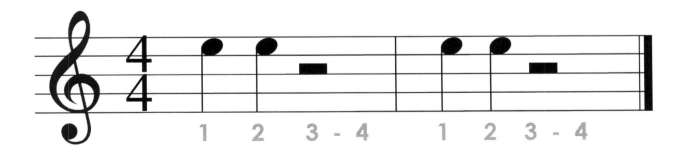

E note

Remember to count. 1-2-3-4, 1-2-3-4.
It is okay to count out loud.
Count two for the half notes and four
for the whole notes.

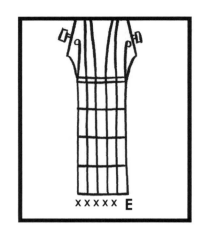

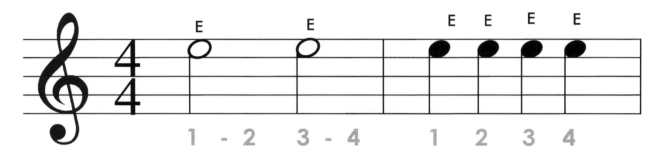

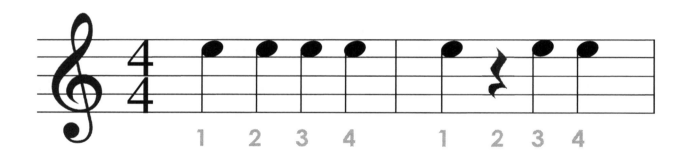

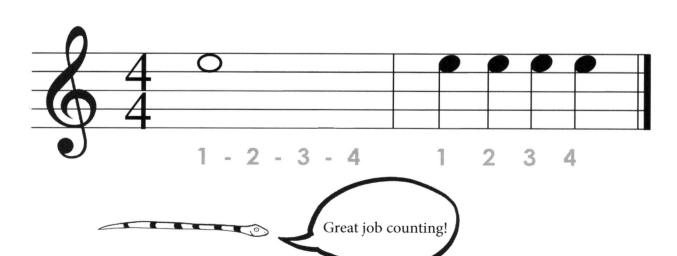

F note

Let's practice playing the F note. Put your first finger on the first fret of the first string, Count out loud. 1-2-3-4, 1-2-3-4. Remember, the rest means you don't play a note.

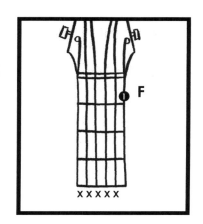

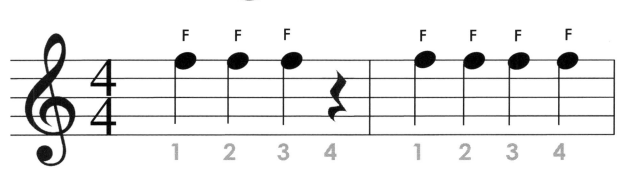

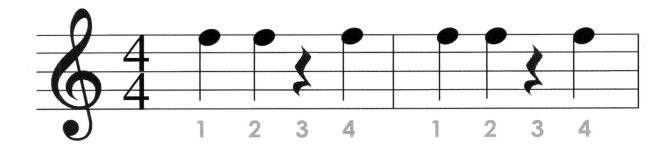

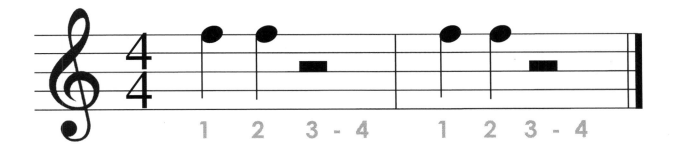

F note

Remember to count. 1-2-3-4, 1-2-3-4.
It is okay to count out loud.
Count two for the half notes and four
for the whole notes.

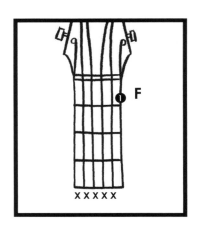

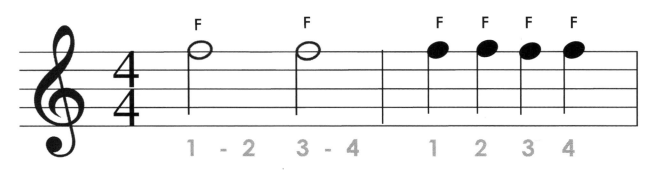

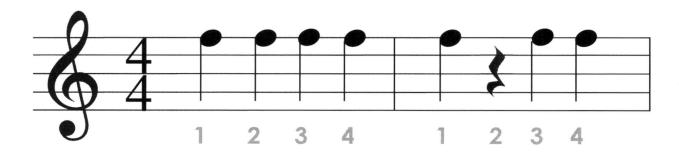

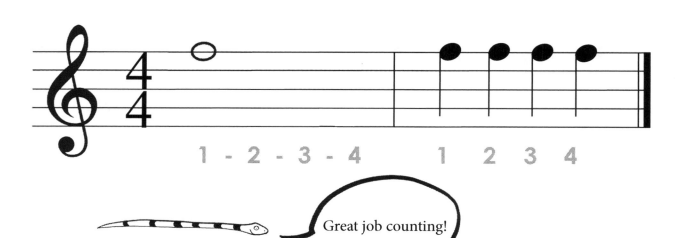

E and F note

Let's practice playing the E and F note. Count out loud. 1-2-3-4. Remember the rest means you don't play a note.

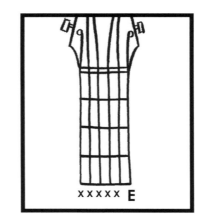

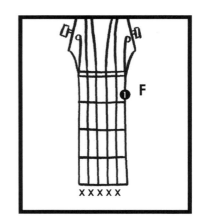

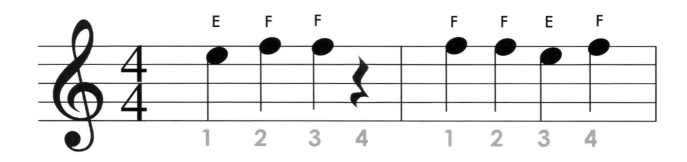

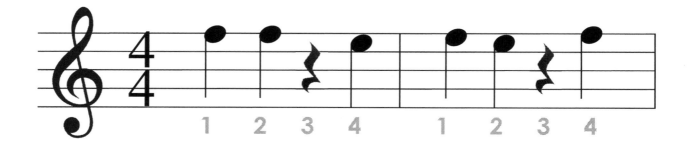

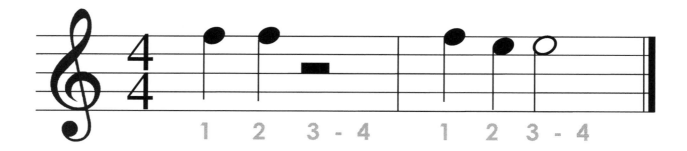

E and F note

Remember, the F note is the first finger on the first fret of the first string. The E is an open string.

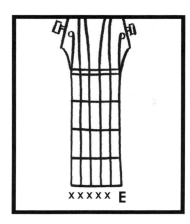

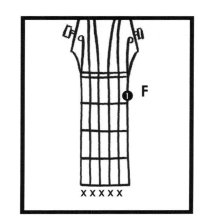

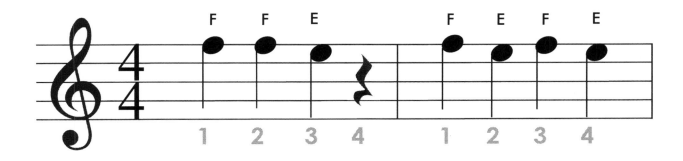

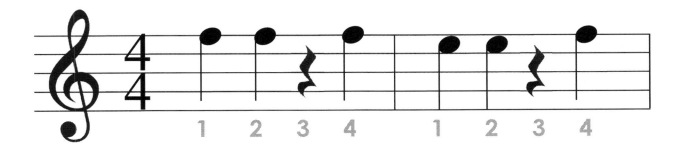

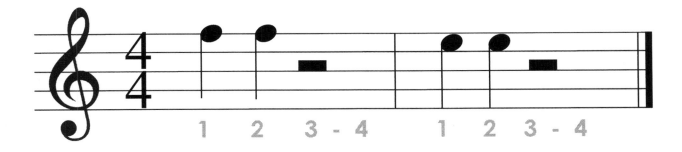

E and F note

Count out loud.
1-2-3-4, 1-2-3-4, 1-2-3-4,
1-2-3-4, 1-2-3-4.

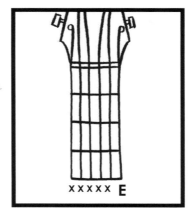
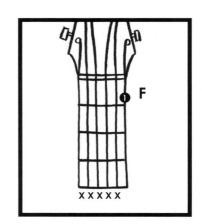

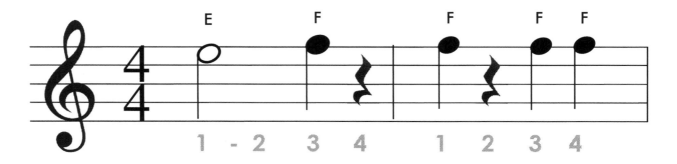

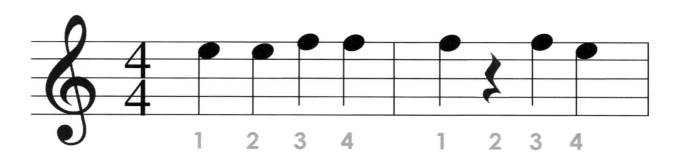

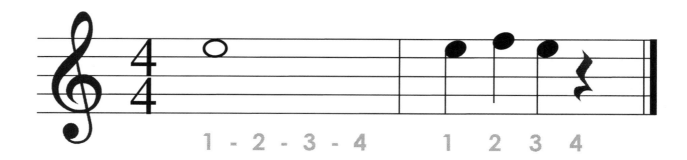

E and F note

You are doing a great job counting. Remember to use the tip of your finger when you hold down the string.

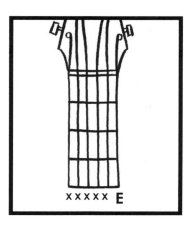

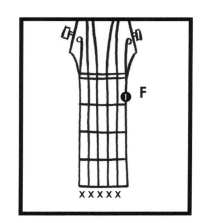

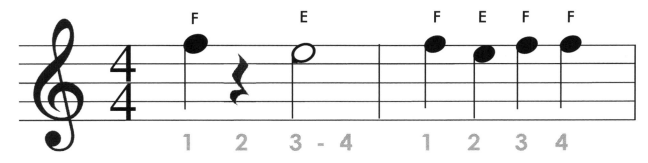

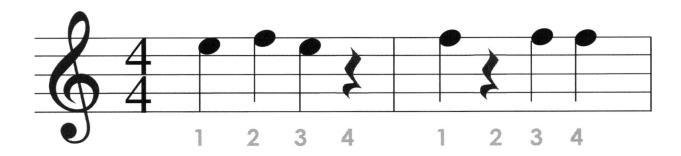

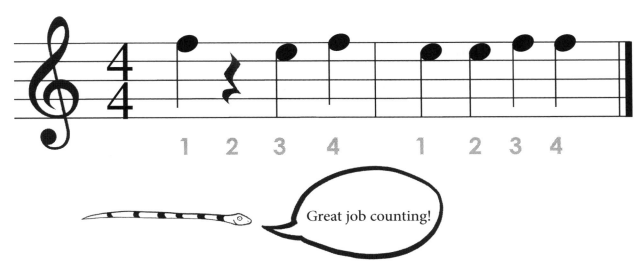

Great job counting!

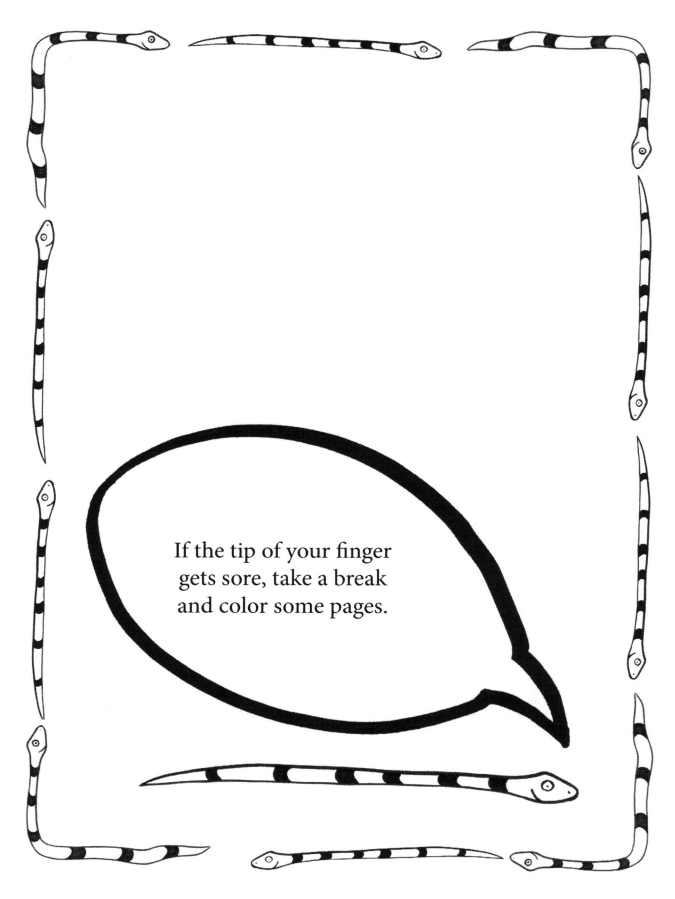

If the tip of your finger gets sore, take a break and color some pages.

G note

Let's practice playing the G note now. Place your third finger on the third fret on the first string. There are 4 beats in one measure. Count out loud. 1-2-3-4, 1-2-3-4, 1-2-3-4.

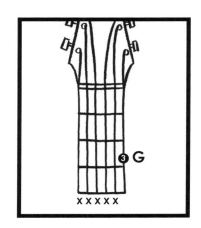

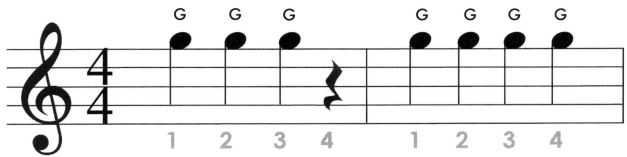

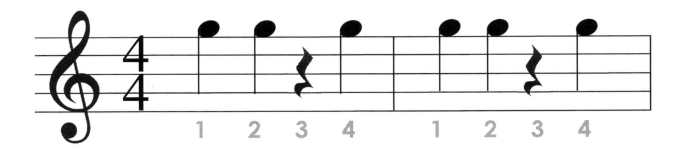

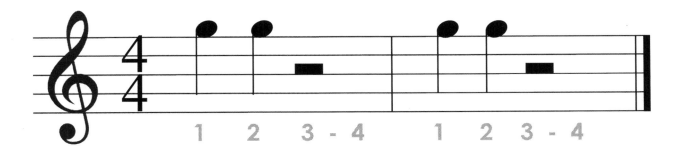

G note

There are 4 beats in one measure. Count out loud. 1-2-3-4, 1-2-3-4, 1-2-3-4. The rest means you don't play a note.

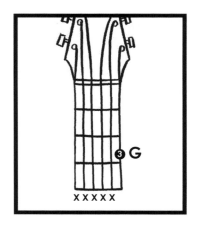

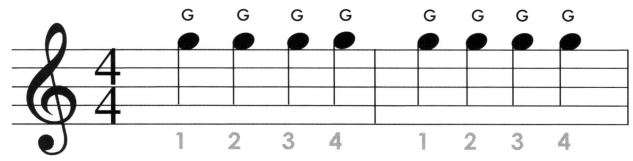

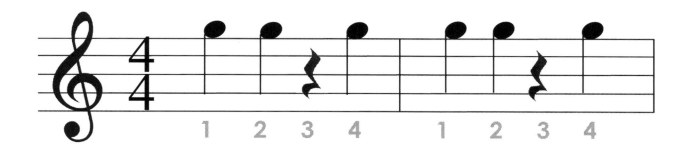

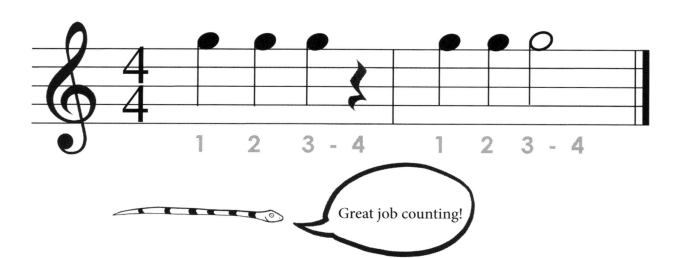

G note

Remember to count! There are 4 beats in one measure. Count out loud. 1-2-3-4, 1-2-3-4, 1-2-3-4. The rest means you don't play a note.

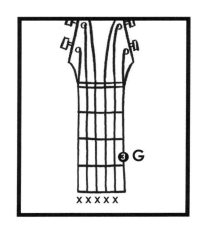

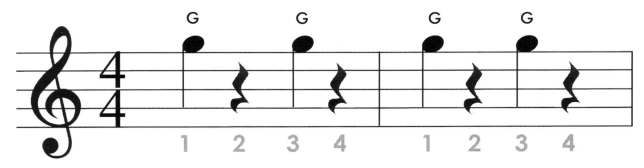

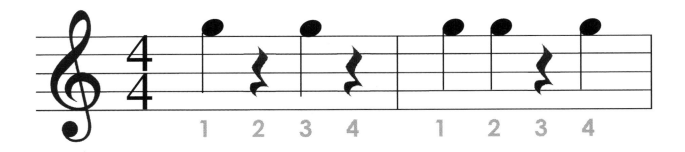

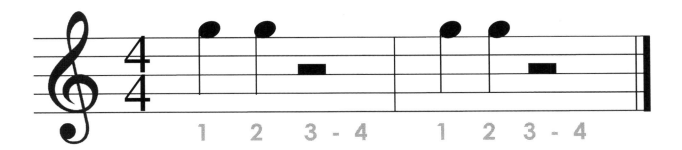

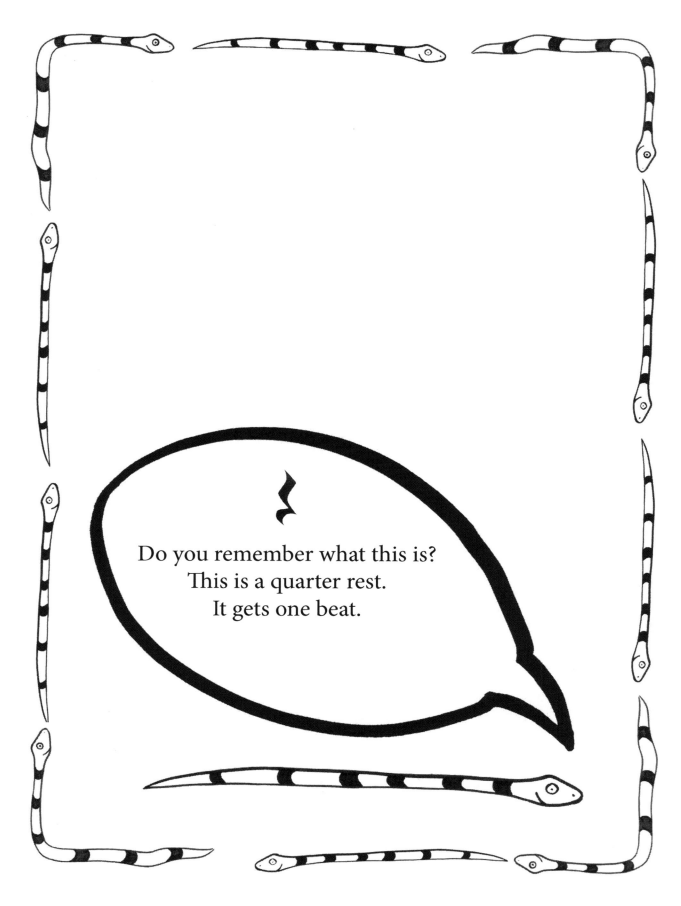

3 note exercise:

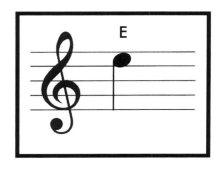 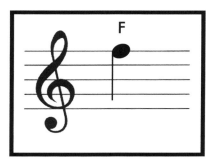 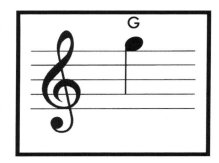

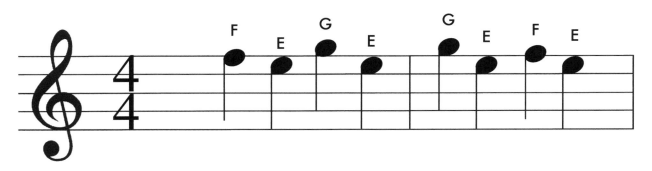

Let's play all three notes together now. Remember to use the correct finger to play the notes. The first finger is for the F note, and the third finger is for the G note

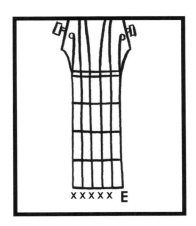 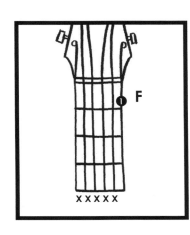 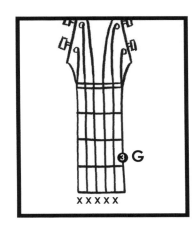

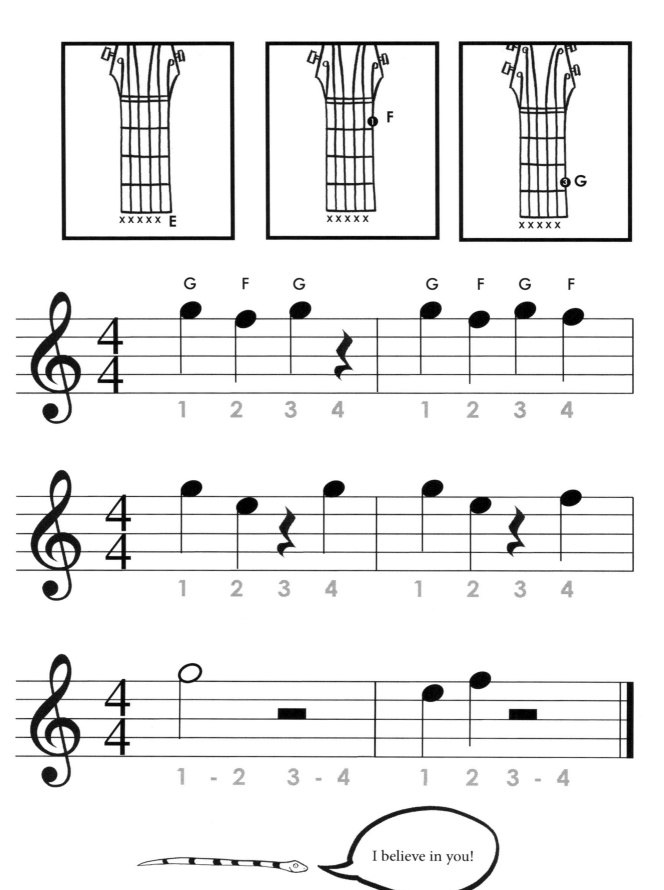

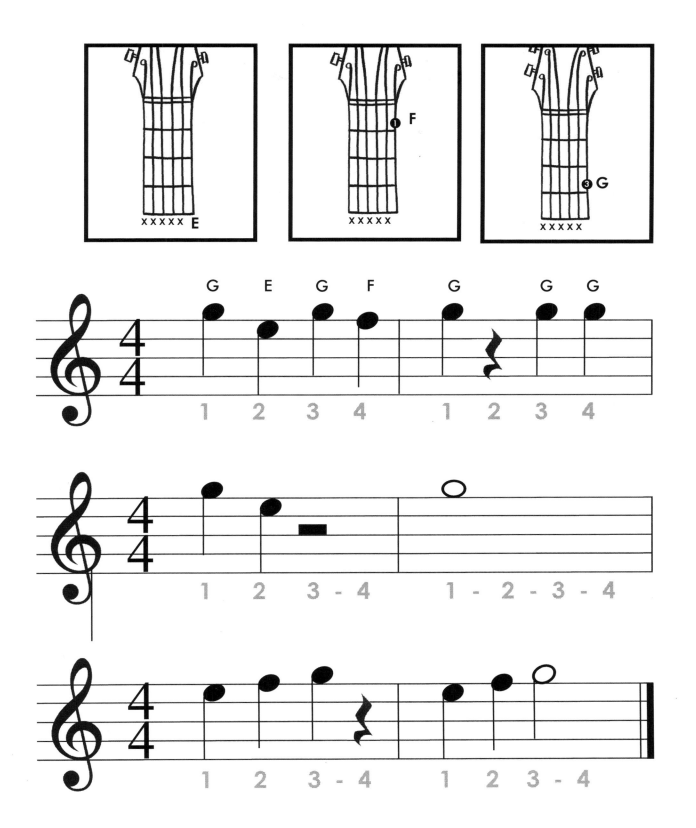

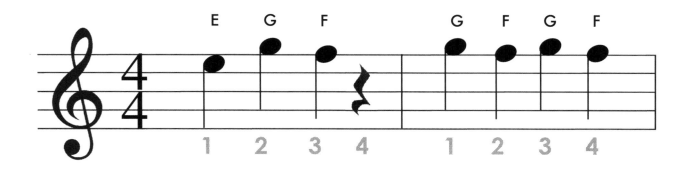

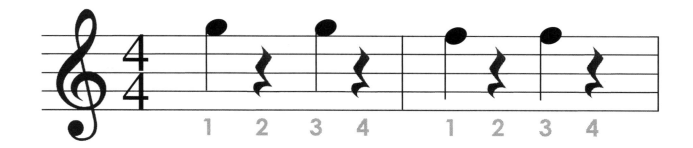

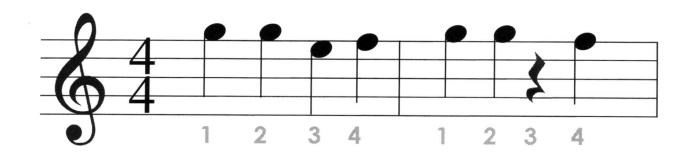

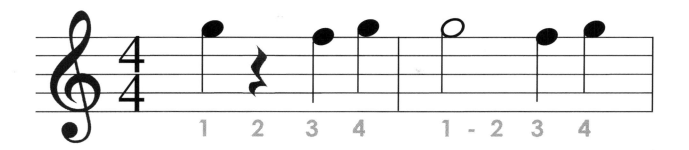

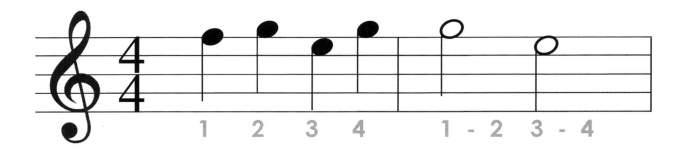

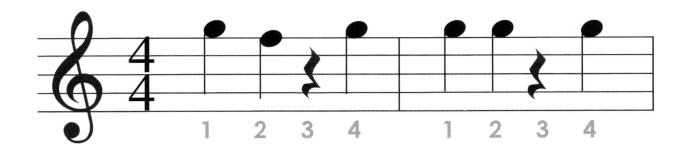

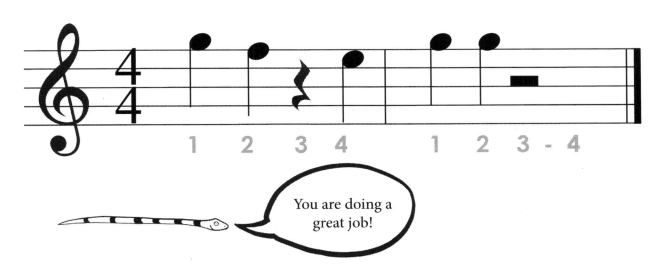

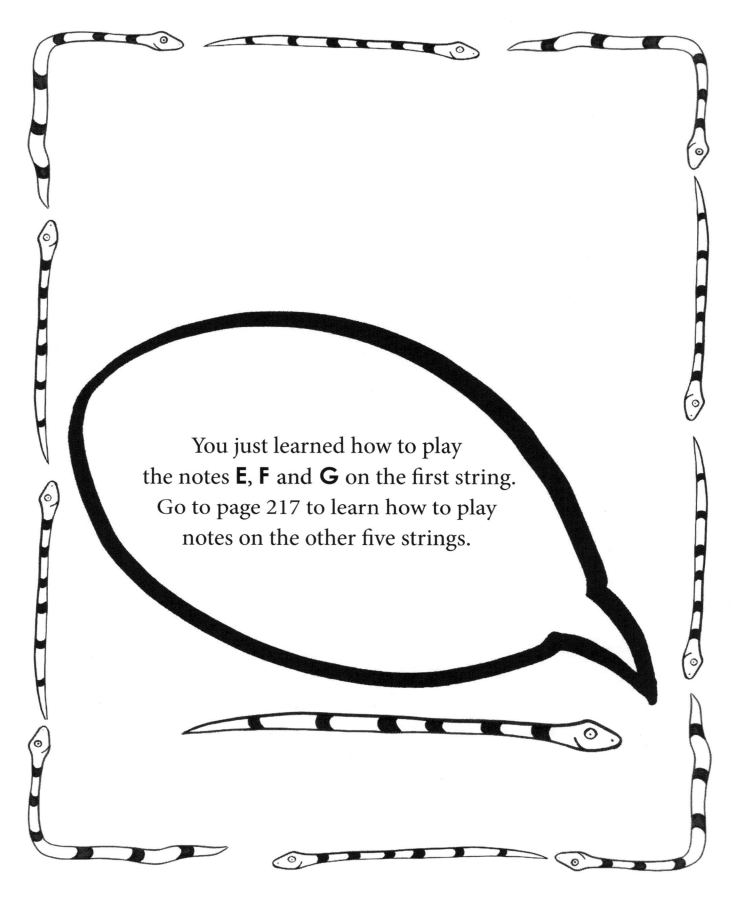

You just learned how to play
the notes **E**, **F** and **G** on the first string.
Go to page 217 to learn how to play
notes on the other five strings.

Make up an exercise:

Write your own music with the three notes you just learned how to play, **E**, **F** and **G**, the notes played on the first string. You can use quarter notes, half notes whole notes and rests. Remember, there are four beats per measure.

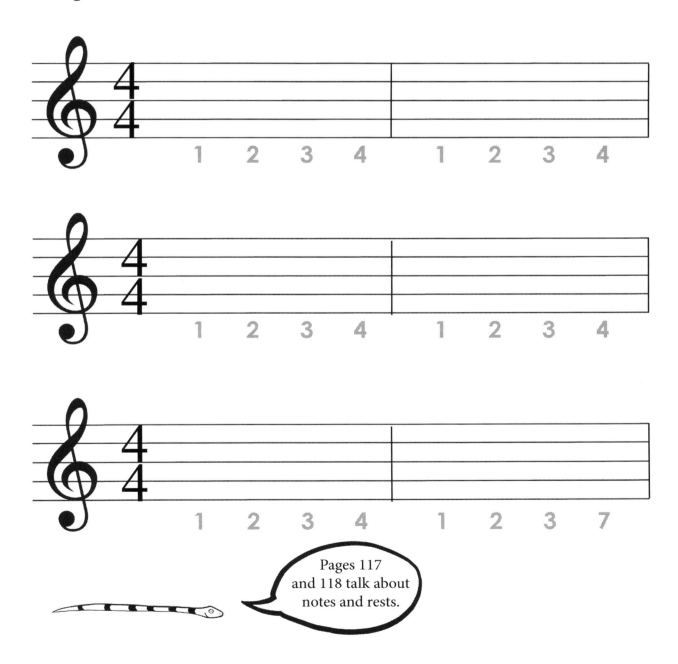

Pages 117 and 118 talk about notes and rests.

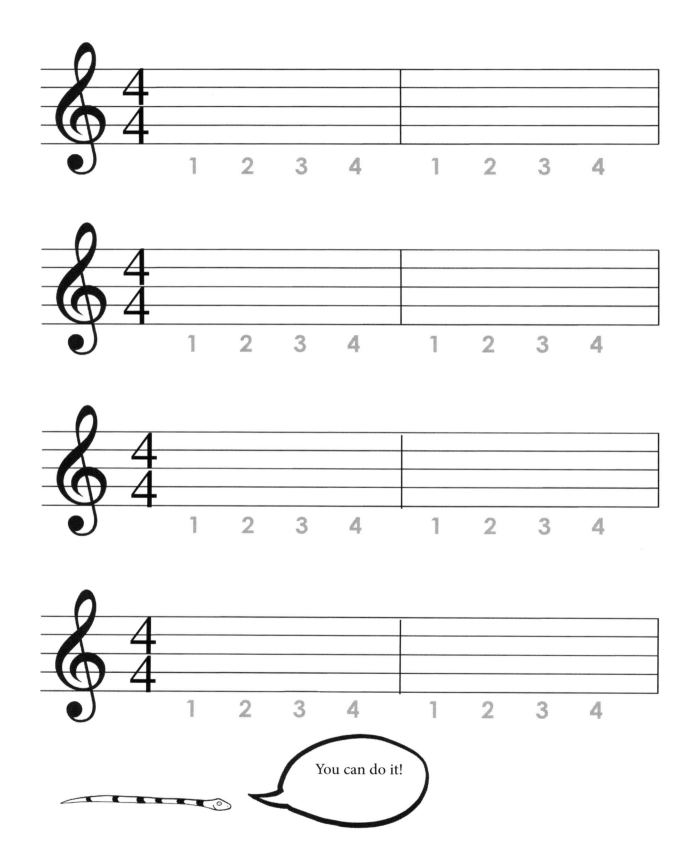

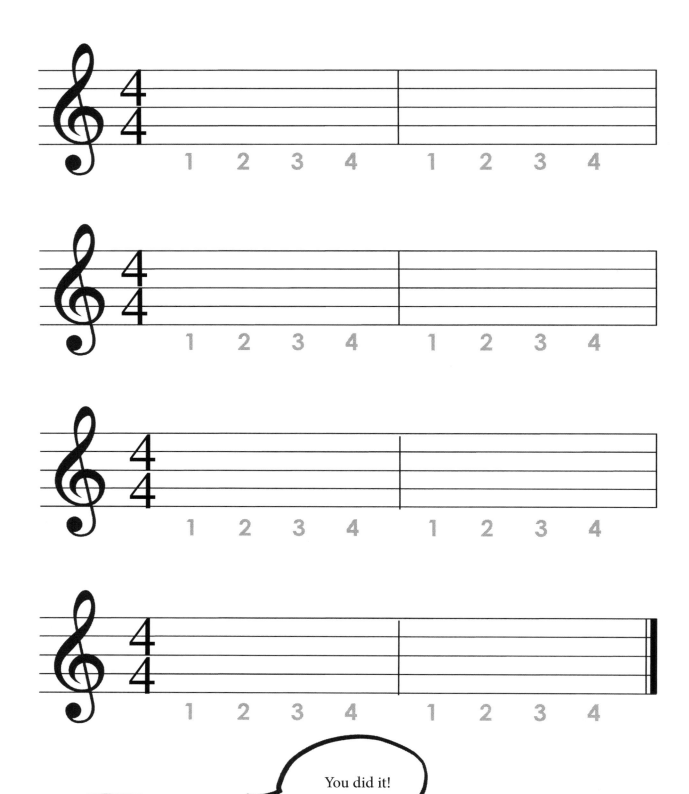

Strumming

Let's learn how to strum your guitar!

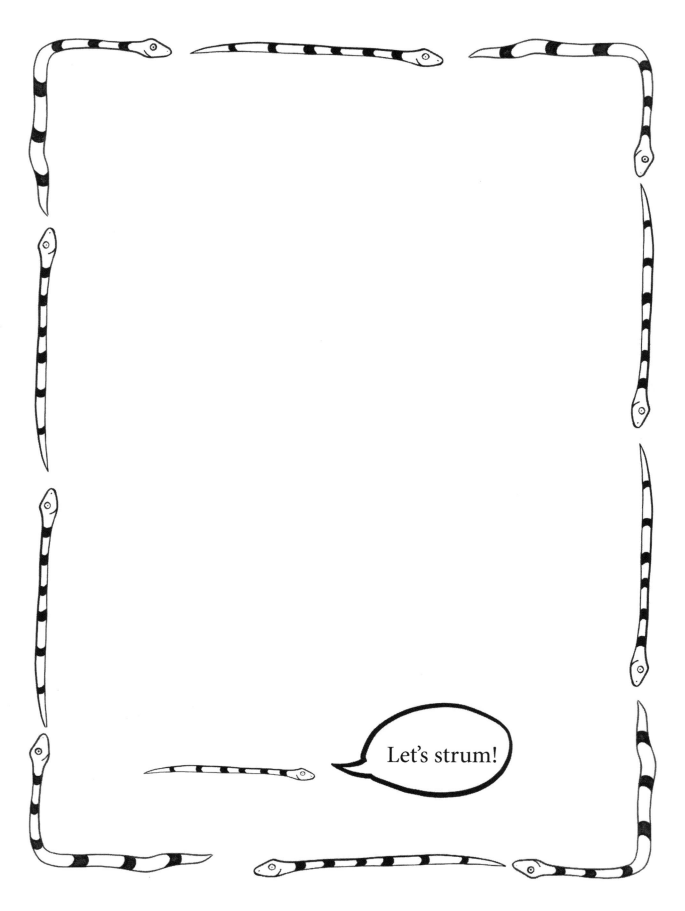

Learning to strum

In this exercise you will learn how to strum the strings on your guitar.

Hold the guitar close into your body, resting it on your leg, while sitting on a chair. Drape the top half of your arm (shoulder to elbow) over the front half of your guitar. The top half of your arm will remain still and stuck to the guitar like glue. From your elbow to your wrist it will swing like a pendulum.

With one hand behind the neck of the guitar, use your other hand or thumb to play the strings. Start at the sixth string, the thickest string, and with a relaxed hand, glide your thumb down the strings, trying to play each string equally.

/ This is the symbol we will use to indicate a downward strum, from large strings to small strings.

V This is the symbol we will use to indicate an upward strum, from small strings to large strings.

Where to strum

Strum over the sound hole with a downward strum, then try strumming below the sound hole in different places between the sound hole and the bridge.

You will hear different sounds when you strum in different places on the strings. Over the sound hole will sound deeper, and closer to the bridge will have a higher pitched sound.

Practice strumming on each string equally so you get one big sound; if you go too slowly you hear each string individually.

Practice strumming up and down. Try tapping your feet to help you keep the beat!

It may be loud.
But loud is okay.
Play what's in your heart.
Play it proud!
Strum! Strum! Strum!

SOUND HOLE

BRIDGE

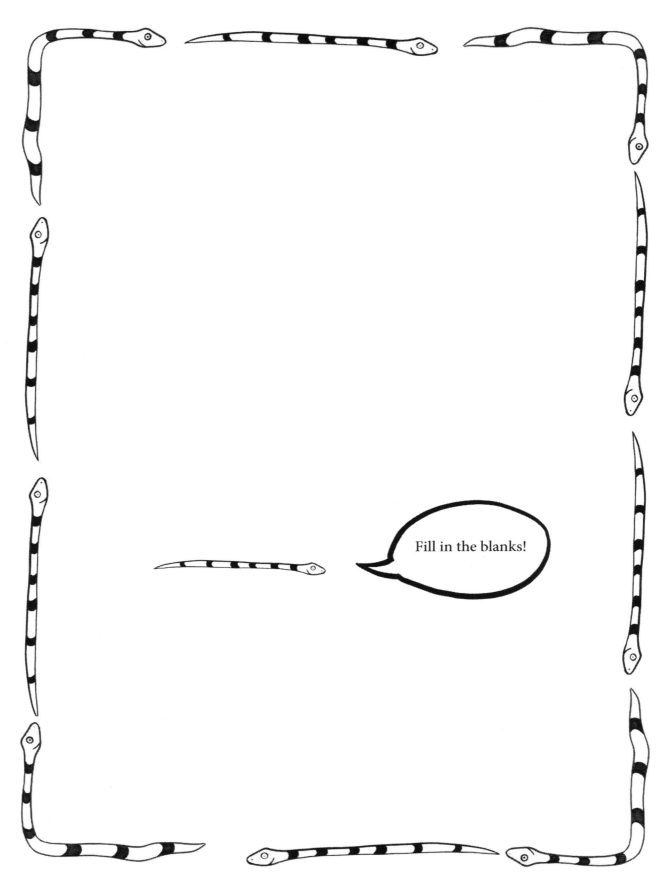

What does it sound like?
Imagining sounds:

When you close your eyes and strum the strings...
What do you see?
The color red or blue?
Or Saturn and its rings?
What about a moon made of cheese?

In the box below, draw a picture of the sounds you make.

Another page to color!

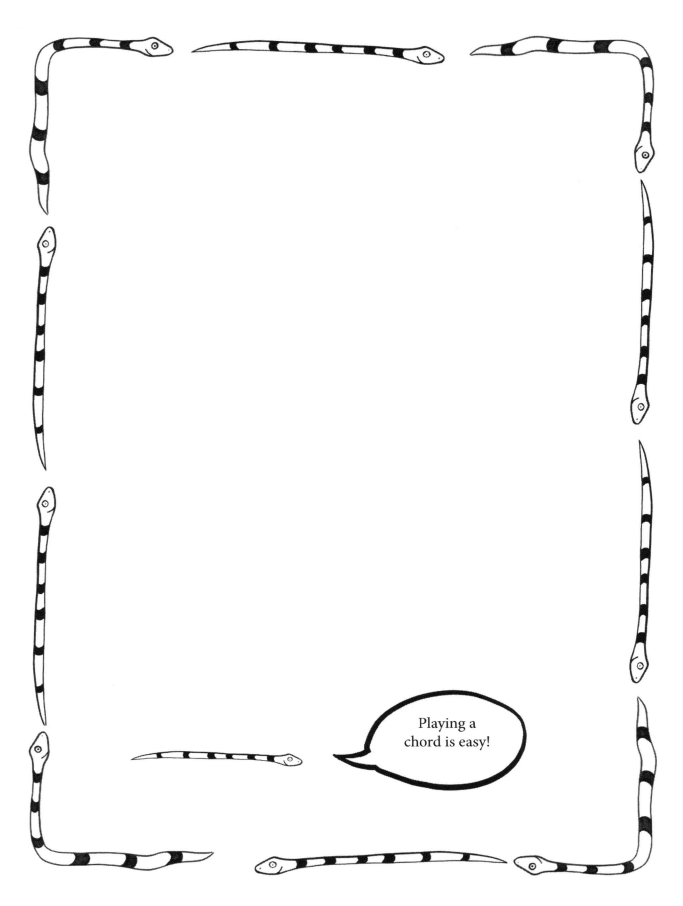

Chords

Let's learn how to strum playing a chord!

Chords

Playing a chord is easy!

A chord is more than one note played at a time, a succession of notes played together. These variations of chords are some of the simplest to learn. They are especially good for any beginner with small hands.

(Look in the back, on page 235, for more chords to learn.)

All chords are written on a chord diagram, similar to earlier pictures of the open strings. The number shown is the finger you will use for that string. The **X** indicates a string you do not play. The **O** indicates the open string.

When playing chords, you glide your pick or fingers across the strings that are open, as well as the strings you hold down with the fingers of your left hand.

G chord:

G chord

Put your third finger on the third fret of the first string. Strum the last four strings at the same time D-G-B-E

This chord has been modified for beginners. The advanced chord is on page 240.

We will count four beats per measure.

A **measure** is the section on a musical staff between two bar lines. A **double bar** at the end of a staff is the end of the piece of music.

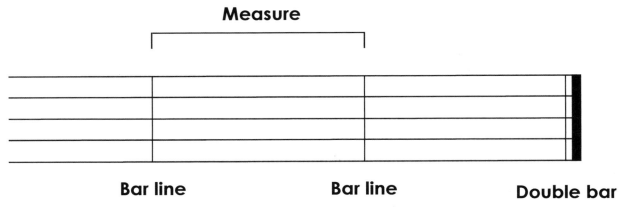

Measure

Bar line   **Bar line**   **Double bar**

Rests

A rest means you don't play a note. You count silently.

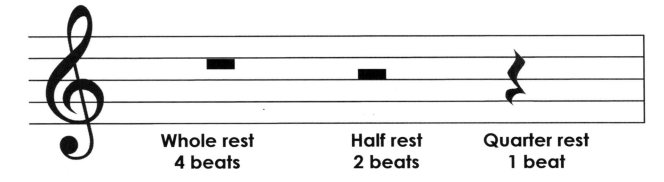

Whole rest   **Half rest**   **Quarter rest**
4 beats   **2 beats**   **1 beat**

G chord

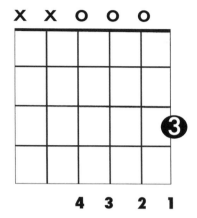

Strum from the fourth string down, playing the **G** chord. This is the symbol for a down strum: /

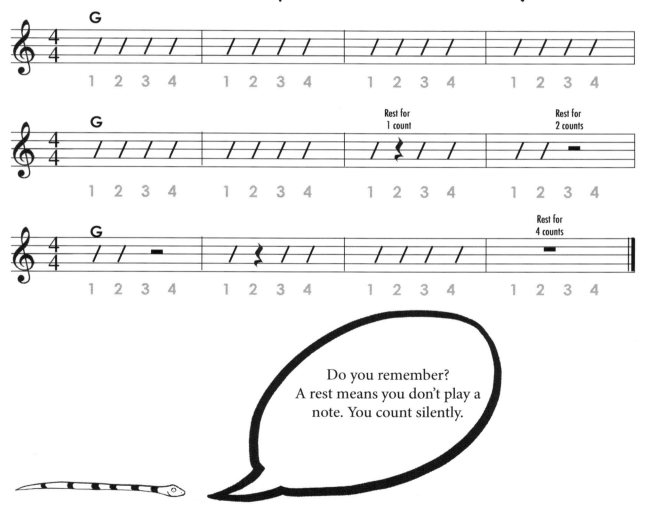

Do you remember? A rest means you don't play a note. You count silently.

G chord

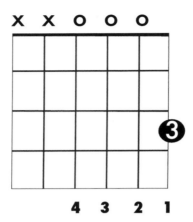

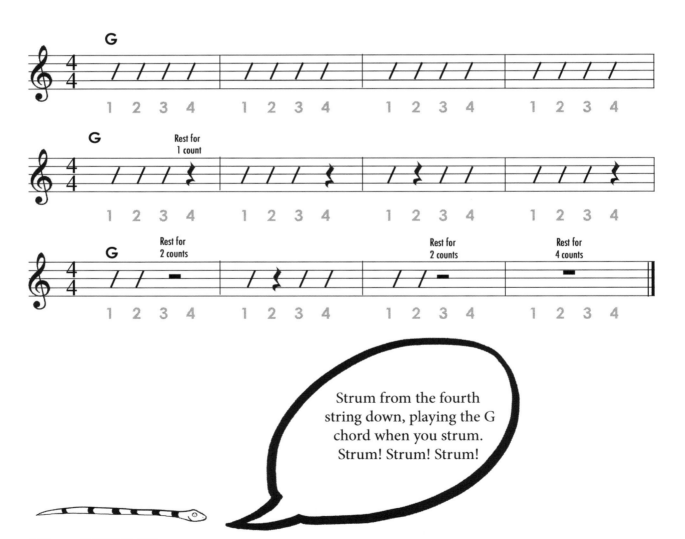

G chord

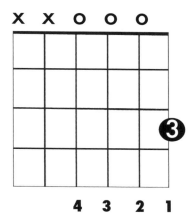

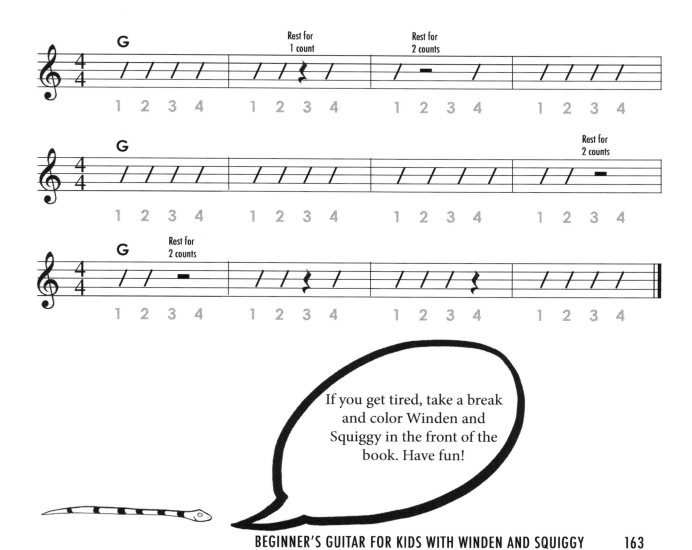

Remember to use the tip
of your fingers to hold down the strings.
Keep your fingernails short!

C chord:

C chord

x x x o o

3 2 1

With **C**, all you need is the first finger on the first fret of the second string (B). Strum from the third string (G) down and leave the first string open.

Let's try it!
Remember,
X = Do not strum.
O = Open string - don't hold it down!

This chord has been modified for beginners. The advanced chord is on page 237.

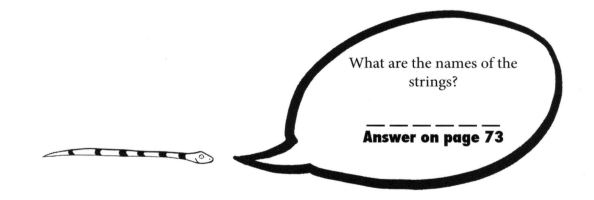

What are the names of the strings?

_____

Answer on page 73

C chord

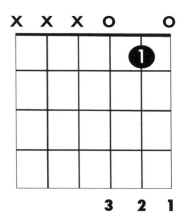

Strum from the third string down, playing the **C** chord. This is the symbol for a down strum: **/**

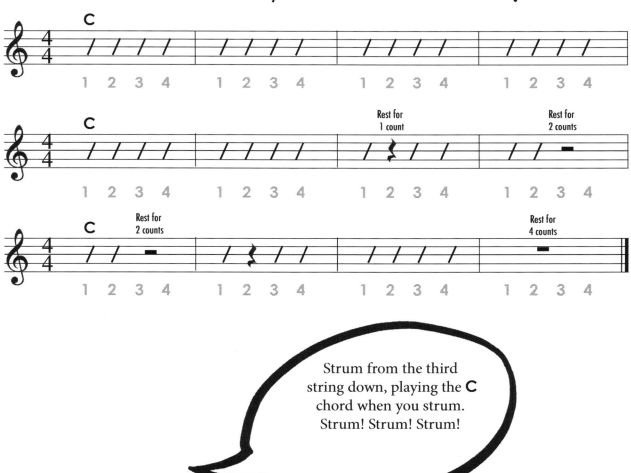

C chord

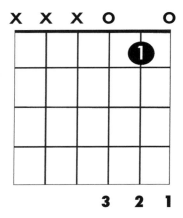

Strum from the third string down, playing the **C** chord. This is the symbol for a down strum: /

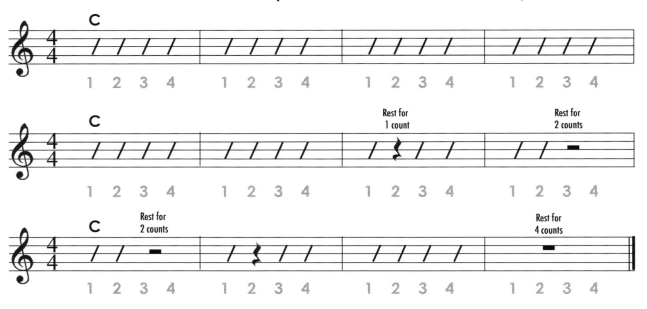

Do you remember?
A rest means you don't play a note. You count silently.

C chord

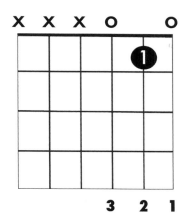

Strum from the third string down, playing the **C** chord. This is the symbol for a down strum: /

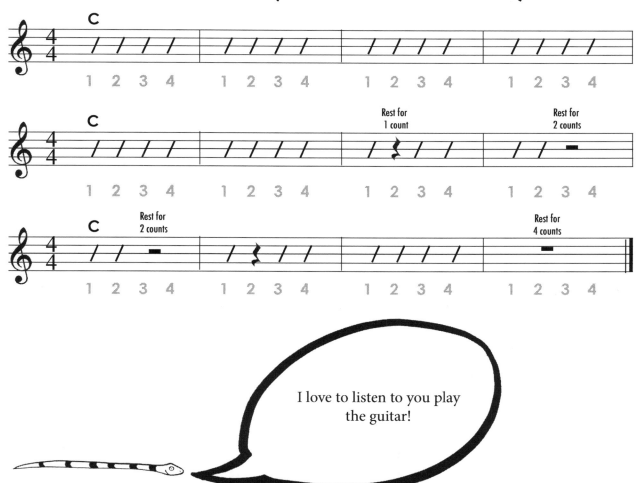

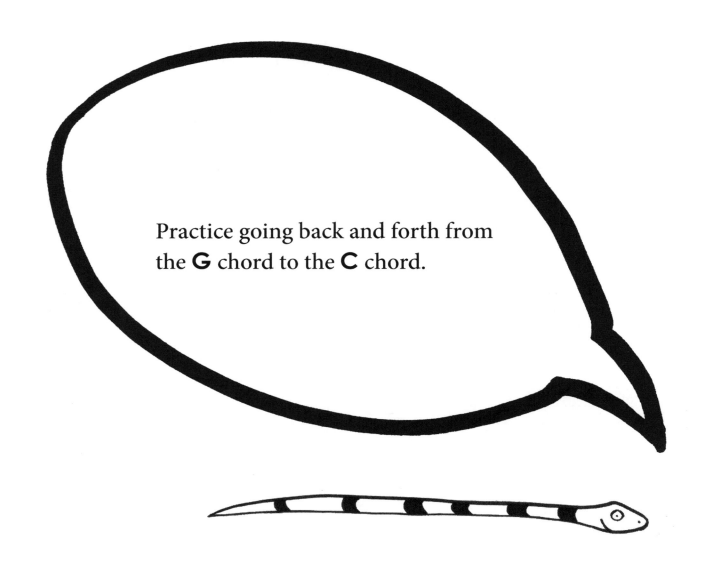

Practice going back and forth from the **G** chord to the **C** chord.

G chord

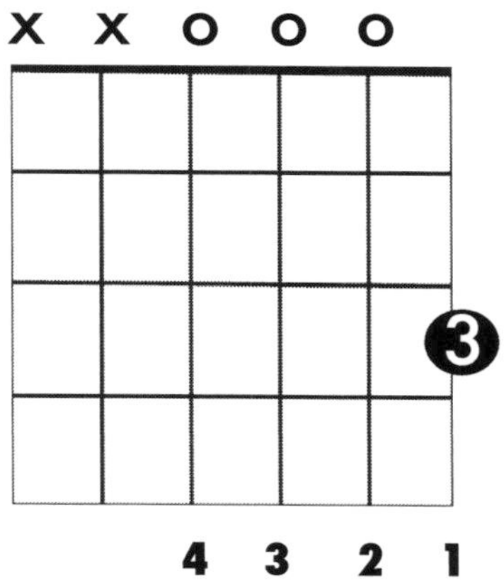
x x o o o
3
4 3 2 1

C chord

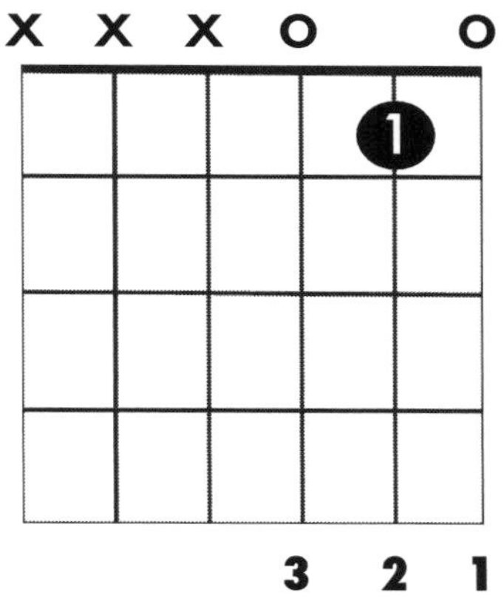
x x x o o
1
3 2 1

Let's play **G** and **C** together. Count out loud!

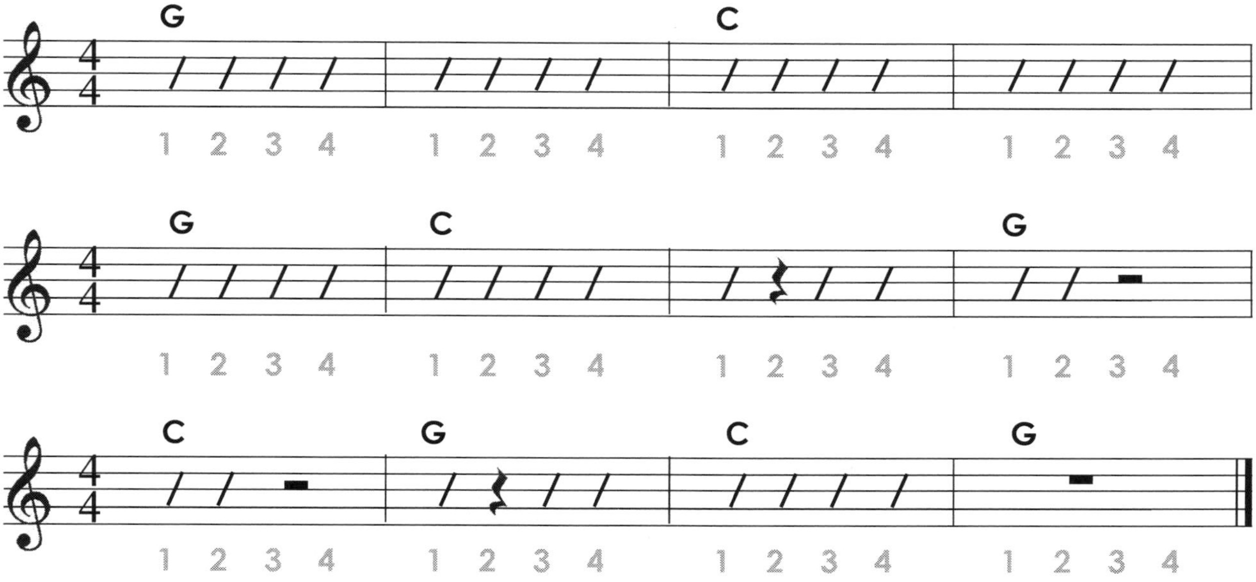
G
C
1 2 3 4 1 2 3 4 1 2 3 4 1 2 3 4
G
C
G
1 2 3 4 1 2 3 4 1 2 3 4 1 2 3 4
C
G
C
G
1 2 3 4 1 2 3 4 1 2 3 4 1 2 3 4

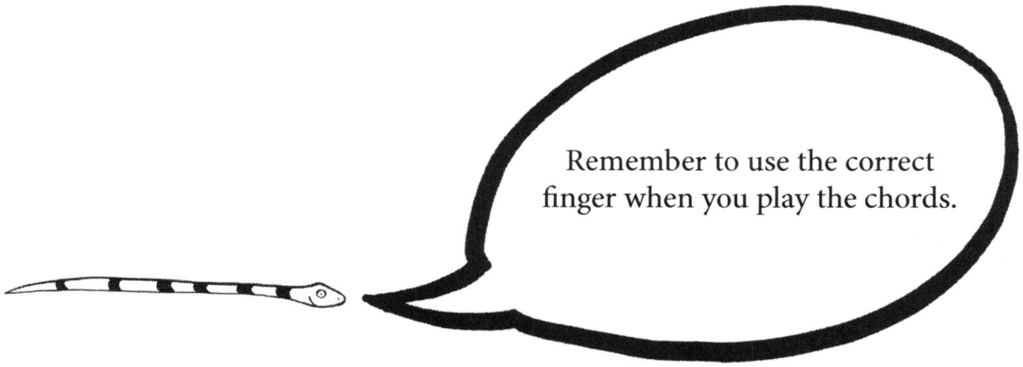
Remember to use the correct finger when you play the chords.

E minor chord:

Em chord

x x   o o o

2

4 3 2 1

The **E minor** chord is especially simple because you only put one finger on the second fret of the fourth (D) string. You strum from the fourth string down to the first string.

This chord has been modified for beginners. The advanced chord is on page 239.

Em chord

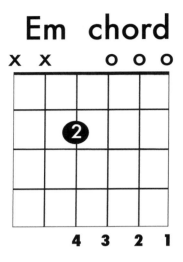

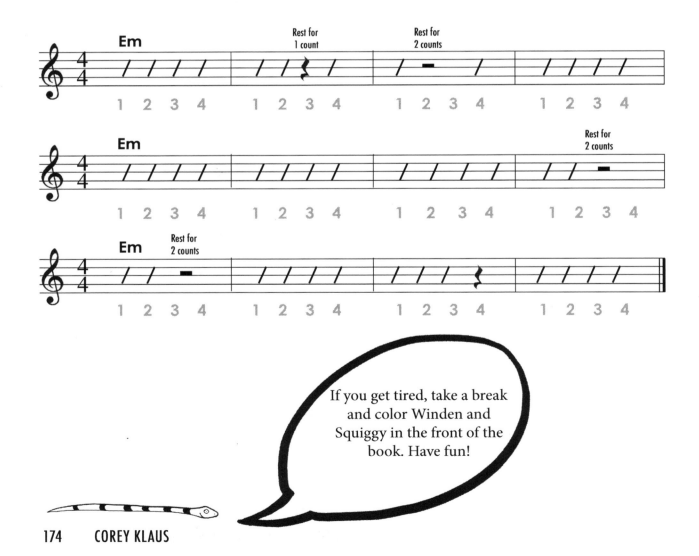

COREY KLAUS

Em chord

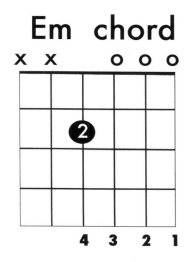

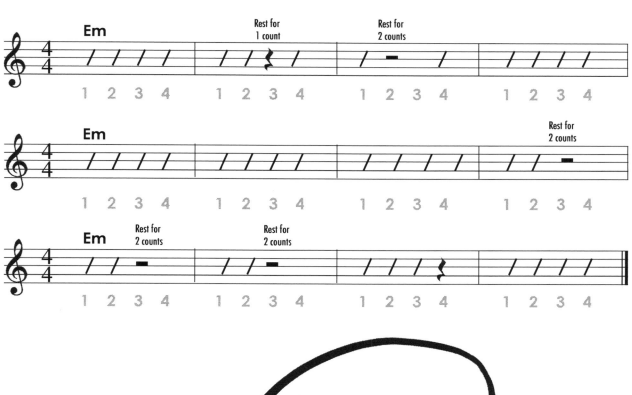

Em chord

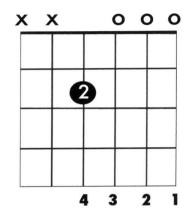

x x   o o o

2

4 3 2 1

C chord

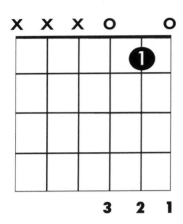

x x x o   o

1

3 2 1

Let's play **Em** and **C** together. Count out loud!

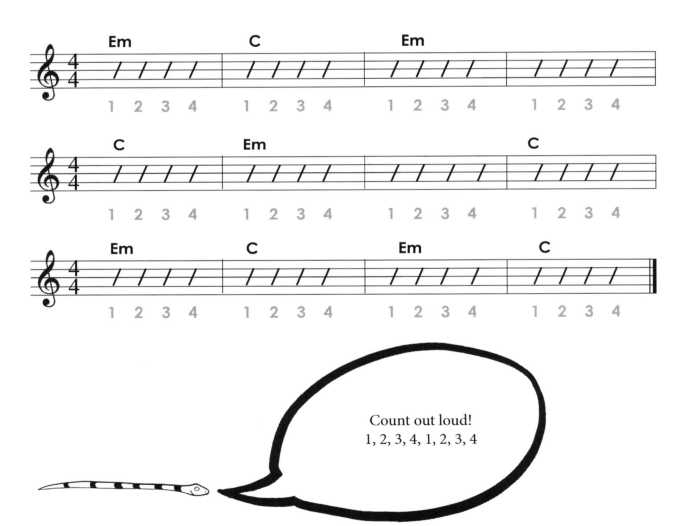

Count out loud!
1, 2, 3, 4, 1, 2, 3, 4

G chord

x x o o o

3

4 3 2 1

C chord

x x x o o

1

3 2 1

Em chord

x x o o o

2

4 3 2 1

Let's try all three! **G**, **C** and **Em** together.

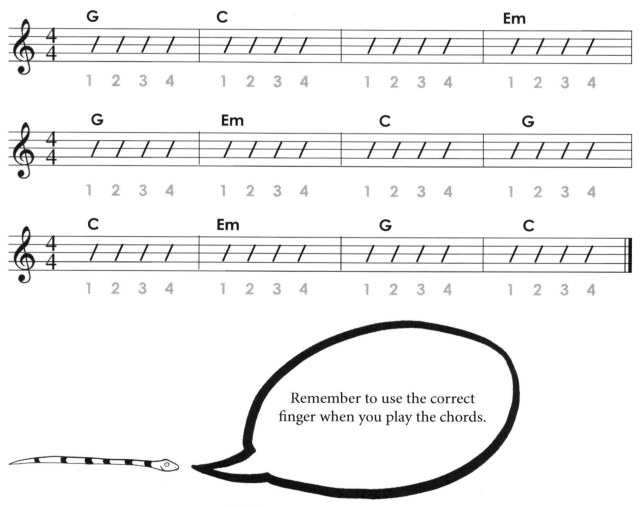

Remember to use the correct finger when you play the chords.

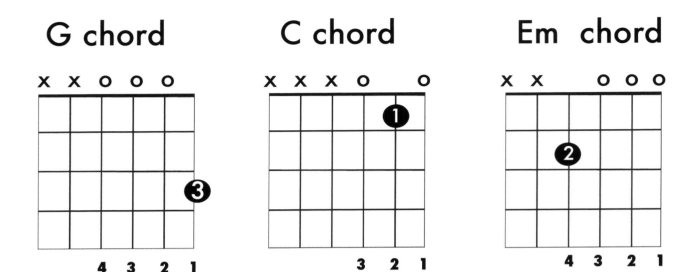

Practice switching between **G**, **C** and **Em**

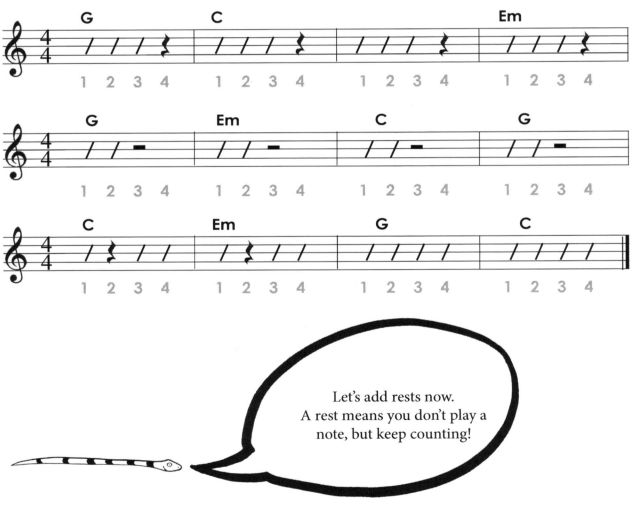

Let's add rests now.
A rest means you don't play a
note, but keep counting!

G chord   C chord   Em chord

x x o o o

4 3 2 1

x x x o o

3 2 1

x x o o o

4 3 2 1

Keep going! You are doing a great job!

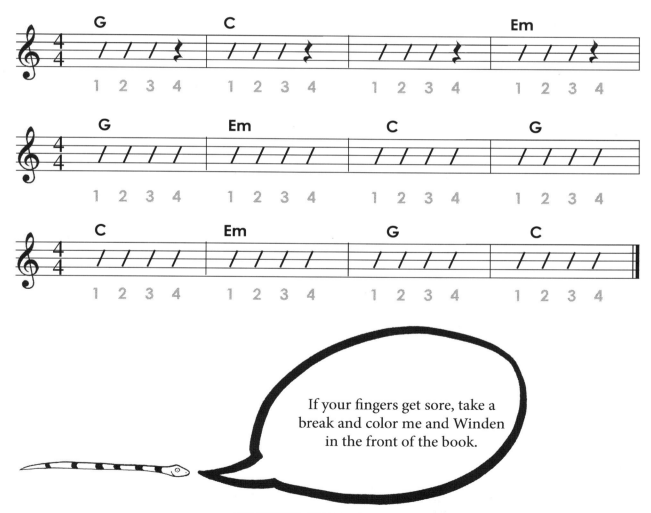

If your fingers get sore, take a break and color me and Winden in the front of the book.

G chord

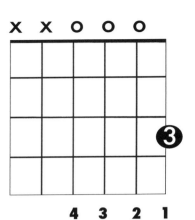

C chord

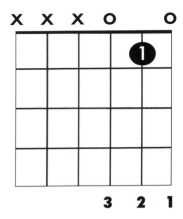

Em chord

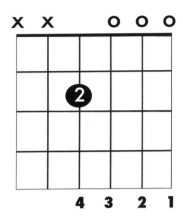

These chords have been modified for beginners. The advanced chords are on page 235.

Chord switching practice
G, C, Em

Strum each chord four times.
Practice switching back and forth. See page 180
if you need help remembering the chords.

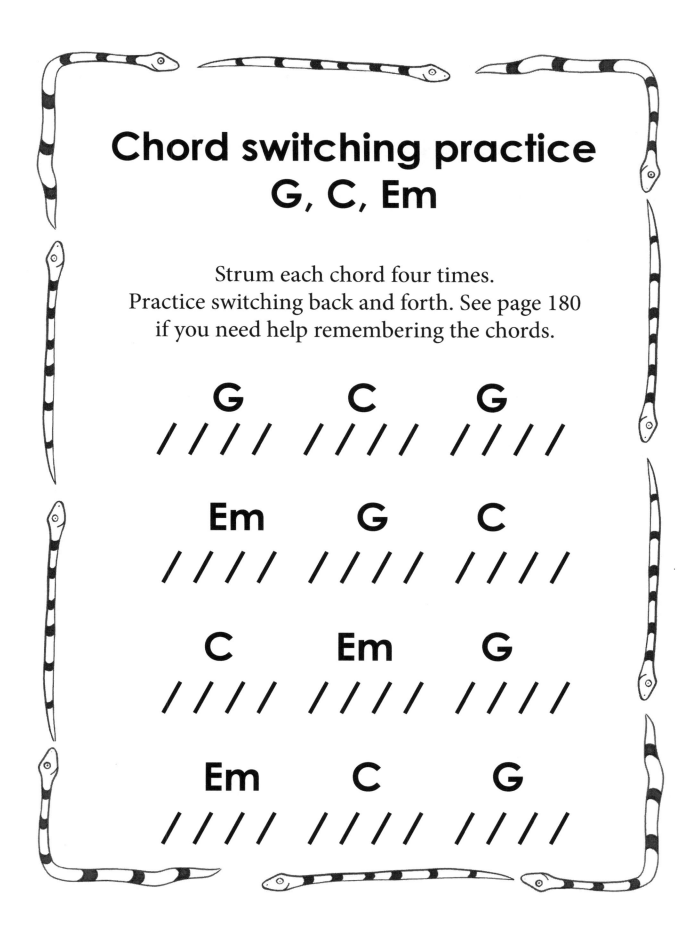

G	C	G
/ / / /	/ / / /	/ / / /

Em	G	C
/ / / /	/ / / /	/ / / /

C	Em	G
/ / / /	/ / / /	/ / / /

Em	C	G
/ / / /	/ / / /	/ / / /

Tempo

Tempo is the speed at which you play; it's the heart-beat of the song. Did you ever notice your heart can speed up or slow down, but it's always there in the background, keeping the song going on and on?

You can start understanding tempo by strumming. To help you keep an even tempo, tap your foot to each beat when you strum. 1, 2, 3, 4, 1, 2, 3, 4 — keep going! 1, 2, 3, 4, 1, 2, 3, 4 ...

To play slower, count: 1 snake, 2 snake, 3 snake, 4 snake, 1 snake, 2 snake, 3 snake, 4 snake.

Make up your own counters!

1 potato, 2 potato, 3 potato, 4 potato, 1 potato, 2 potato, 3 potato, 4 potato ...

Strumming patterns

Let's practice different strumming patterns. I believe in you! You can do it!

G chord

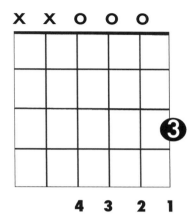

Let's stay with one chord so we can focus on our strumming.

This is the symbol for a down strum: /

This is the symbol for an up strum: V

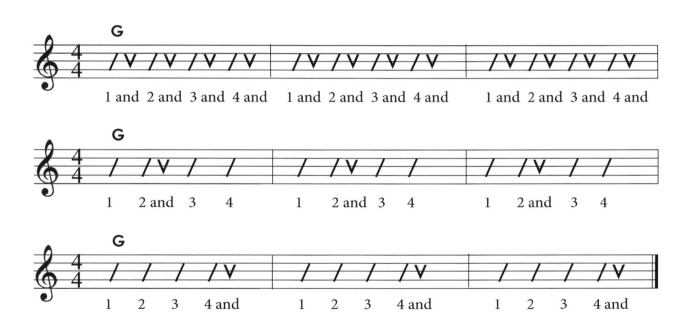

C chord

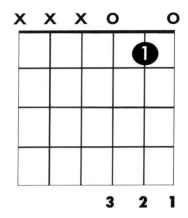

Let's practice strumming patterns with the **C** chord.
This is the symbol for a down strum: **/**
This is the symbol for a up strum: **V**

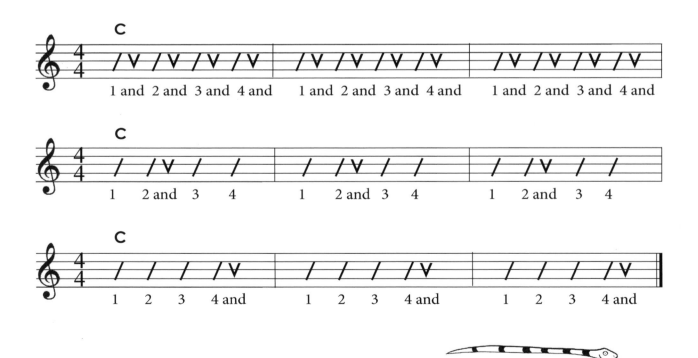

Em chord

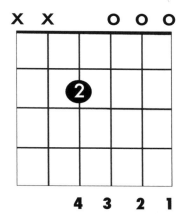

Now let's try practicing the strumming patterns with the **Em** chord.

This is the symbol for a down strum: **/**

This is the symbol for a up strum: **V**

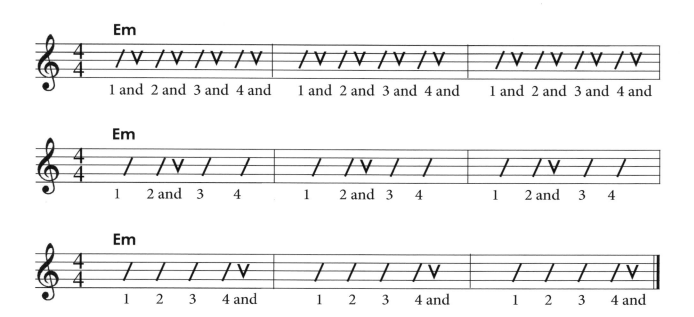

G chord

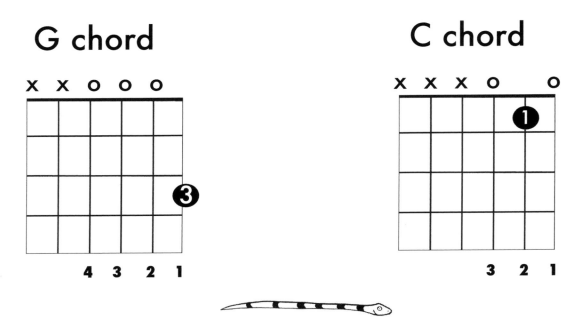

C chord

Let's practice switching between two chords while you learn strumming patterns.

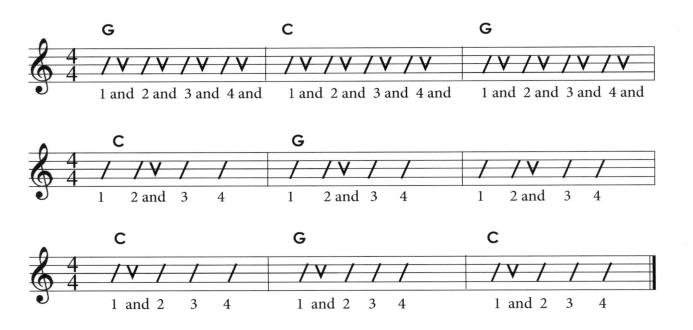

C chord

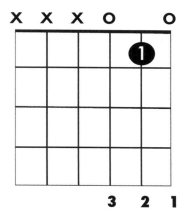

x x x o   o

1

3 2 1

Em chord

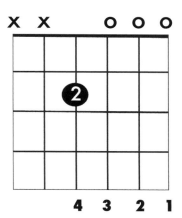

x x   o o o

2

4 3 2 1

Keep practicing the new strumming patterns while switching between chords.

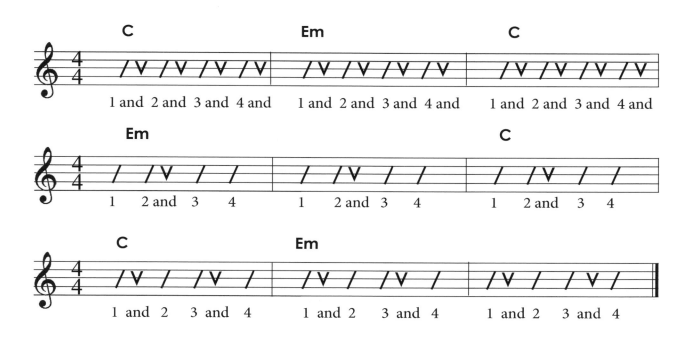

C

Em

C

1 and 2 and 3 and 4 and   1 and 2 and 3 and 4 and   1 and 2 and 3 and 4 and

Em

C

1   2 and 3   4   1   2 and 3   4   1   2 and 3   4

C

Em

1 and 2   3 and 4   1 and 2   3 and 4   1 and 2   3 and 4

Dynamics

It's not always what you play, but how you play. Dynamics are the difference between playing loudly and softly in a piece of music.

Dynamics mean a variation in volume.

Play something quiet when grandpa is napping. Play something loud when you're trying to scare the neighbor's cat next door!

Practice playing loud and soft

The strings will sound louder the harder you hit them. If you touch the strings lightly they will sound softer.

Let's practice playing the strings loud and soft. On the next two pages are the chords you just practiced. Play the pieces again strumming the strings harder, and then play the pieces again, but this time lightly touching the strings.

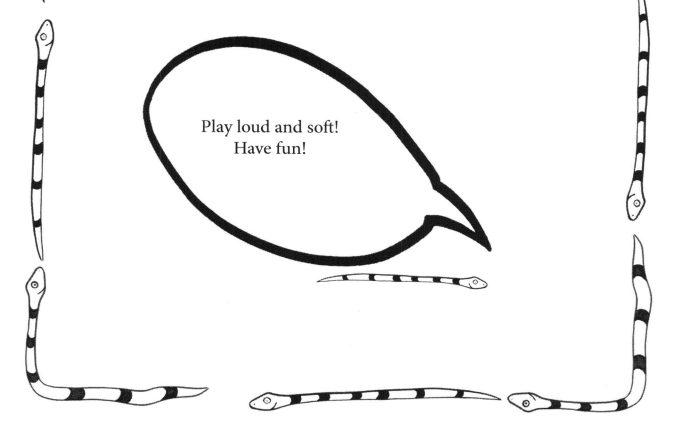

Play loud and soft!
Have fun!

G chord

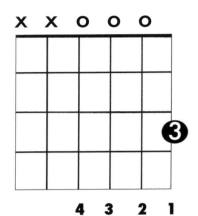

x x o o o

3

4 3 2 1

C chord

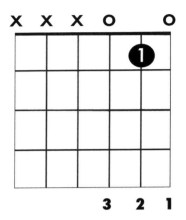

x x x o o

1

3 2 1

Keep practicing switching between two chords while you learn strumming patterns. Try playing the music by hitting the strings harder. Then play the music again and only lightly touch the strings.

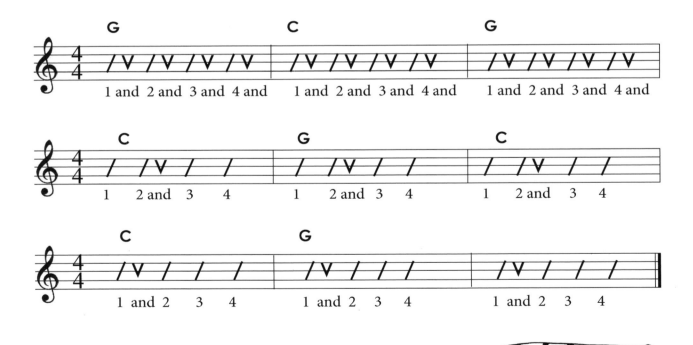

C chord

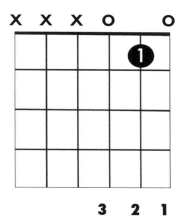

x x x o   o

3   2   1

Em chord

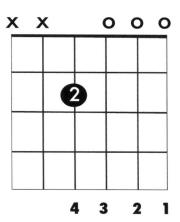

x x   o o o

4   3   2   1

Keep practicing the new strumming patterns while switching between chords. Play the music loud and soft. Dynamics mean a variation in volume.

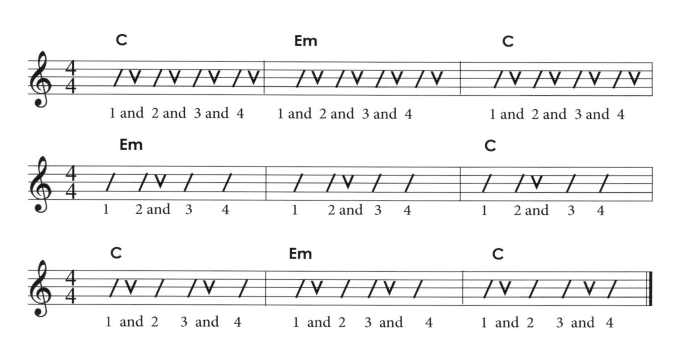

G chord

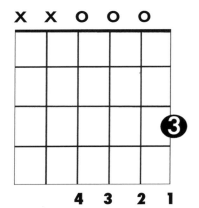

x x o o o

4 3 2 1

C chord

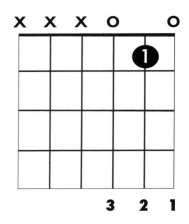

x x x o   o

3 2 1

Em chord

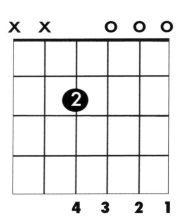

x x   o o o

4 3 2 1

Let's practice switching between three chords.
This is the symbol for a down strum: **/**
This is the symbol for a up strum: **V**

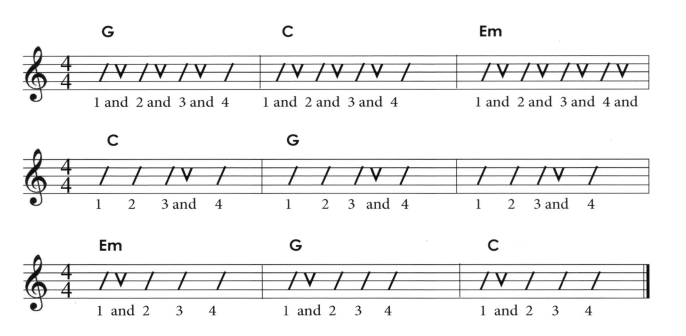

G chord   # C chord   # Em chord

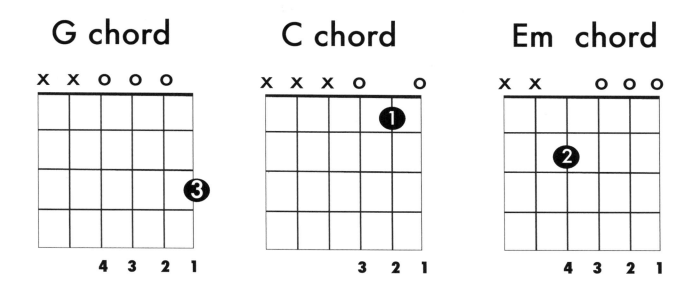

Here are more strumming patterns to practice!
Practice switching between three chords.

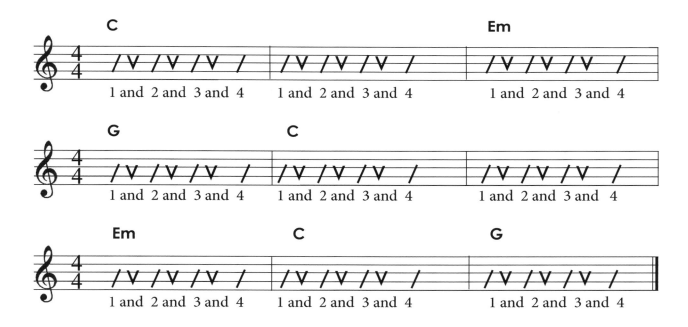

Make your own strumming patterns!

Make your own strumming patterns with the **G**, **C** and **Em** chords. Write above each measure the chord you want to play, and use the down and up marks to make a strumming pattern.

/ = down strum
V = up strum

G chord

x x o o o

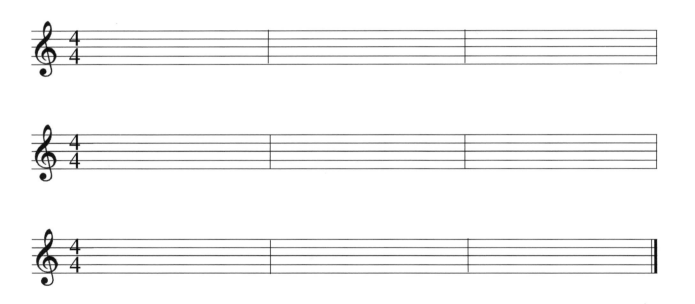

4 3 2 1

C chord

x x x o o

3 2 1

Em chord

x x o o o

4 3 2 1

Make your own strumming patterns, or use one of the patterns you just learned. Write the chord you want to play over each measure.

G chord

x x o o o

3

4 3 2 1

C chord

x x x o o

1

3 2 1

Em chord

x x o o o

2

4 3 2 1

Make your own strumming patterns!
Write the chord you want to play over each measure.

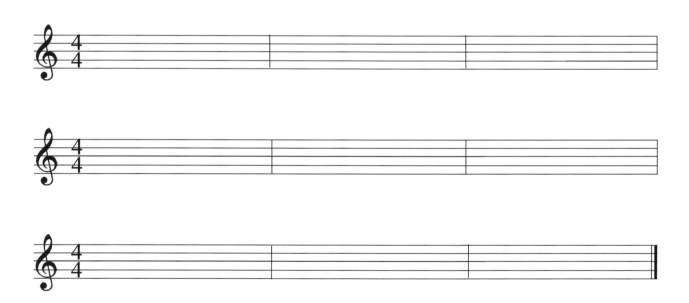

G chord

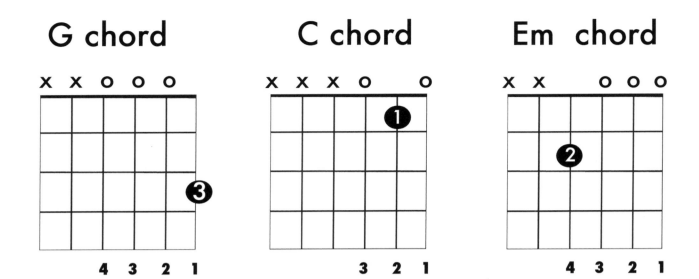

x x o o o

❸

4 3 2 1

C chord

x x x o o

❶

3 2 1

Em chord

x x o o o

❷

4 3 2 1

Make your own strumming patterns!
Write the chord you want to play over each measure.

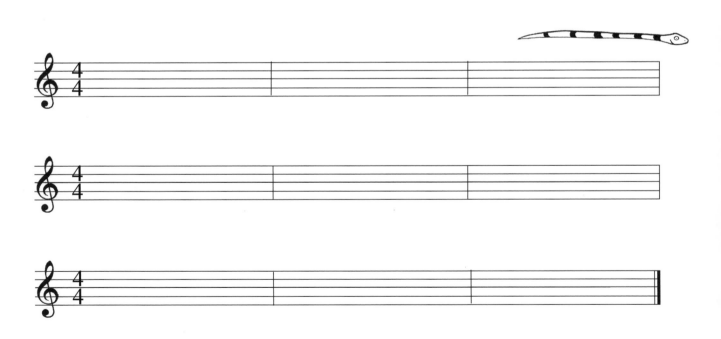

Hey, let's play a song!

On the next two pages are three songs you can play with the chords you just learned. Make up your own strumming patterns to the songs. The songs are in the back of the book with the advanced chords on page 235.

G chord

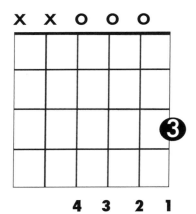

x x o o o

3

4 3 2 1

C chord

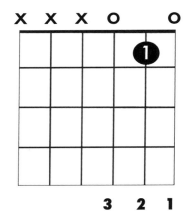

x x x o o

1

3 2 1

Em chord

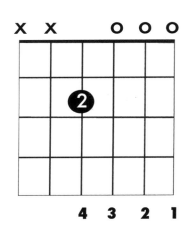

x x o o o

2

4 3 2 1

I Have a Pet Snake

Lyrics by Corey Klaus

G   C   Em
I have a pet snake - it has no arms or legs.

G   C   Em
I named it Squiggy because it likes to play.

Winden and Squiggy

Lyrics by Timber Hodges

G   C
Winden and Squiggy playing the guitar

Em   G
She wants to be a bear, a tree, and a rock star.

G chord

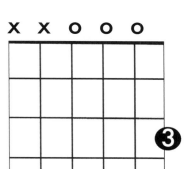

x x o o o

4 3 2 1

C chord

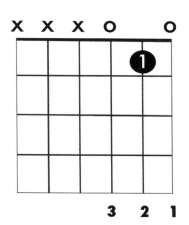

x x x o o

3 2 1

Em chord

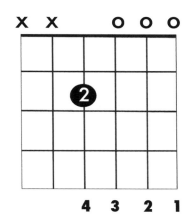

x x o o o

4 3 2 1

Squiggs is my Buddy Buddy

Lyrics by Corey Klaus

<u>C</u>   <u>G</u>
Squiggs is my buddy, buddy. Not some ruddy-duddy

<u>Em</u>   <u>C</u>
Follows me around when I go into town.

<u>G</u>
See him in a tree when he is hiding from me.

<u>C</u>
Tell him to get down when I make this sound.

<u>C</u>
Buddy-Buddy-Buddy, get down buddy,

<u>G</u>   <u>C</u>
Squiggy -iggy-iggs, get down from those twigs.

Hey, let's make a song!

Make your own song! Pick one or two chords you have already learned, or choose new chords starting on page 235. Write above each measure the chord you want to play, and use the down and up marks to make your own strumming pattern.

/ = down strum

V = up strum

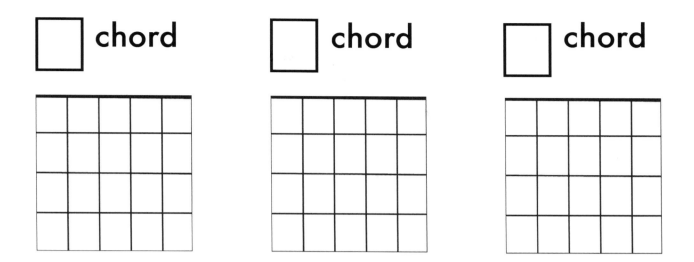

☐ chord   ☐ chord   ☐ chord

Draw your own chord diagrams in the boxes above, and write the chords you want to play over the measures below. Create your own strumming patterns or use the ones you just learned.

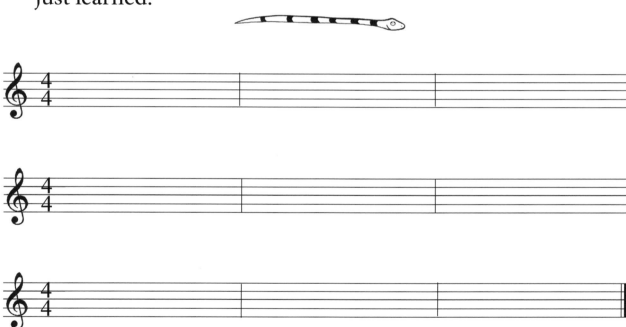

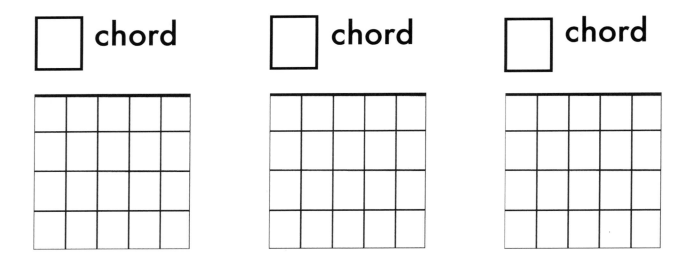

☐ chord   ☐ chord   ☐ chord

Draw your own chord diagrams in the boxes above, and write the chords you want to play over the measures below. Create your own strumming patterns or use the ones you just learned.

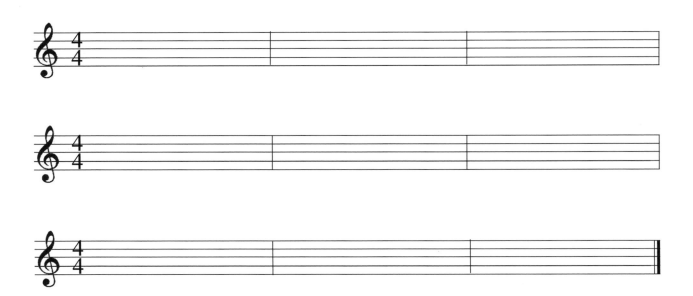

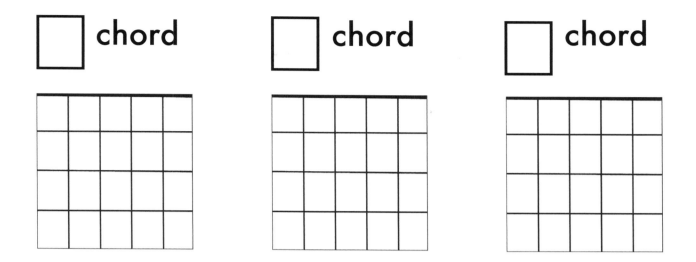

chord   chord   chord

Draw your own chord diagrams in the boxes above, and write the chords you want to play over the measures below. Create your own strumming patterns or use the ones you just learned.

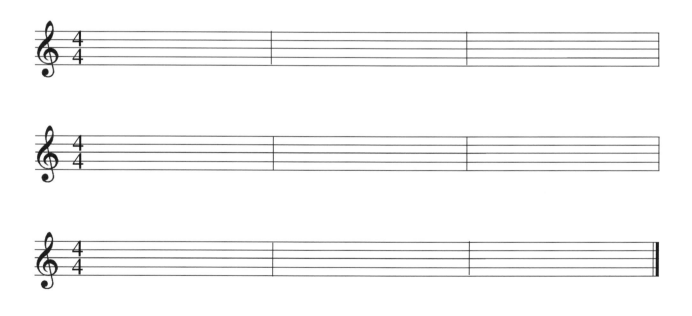

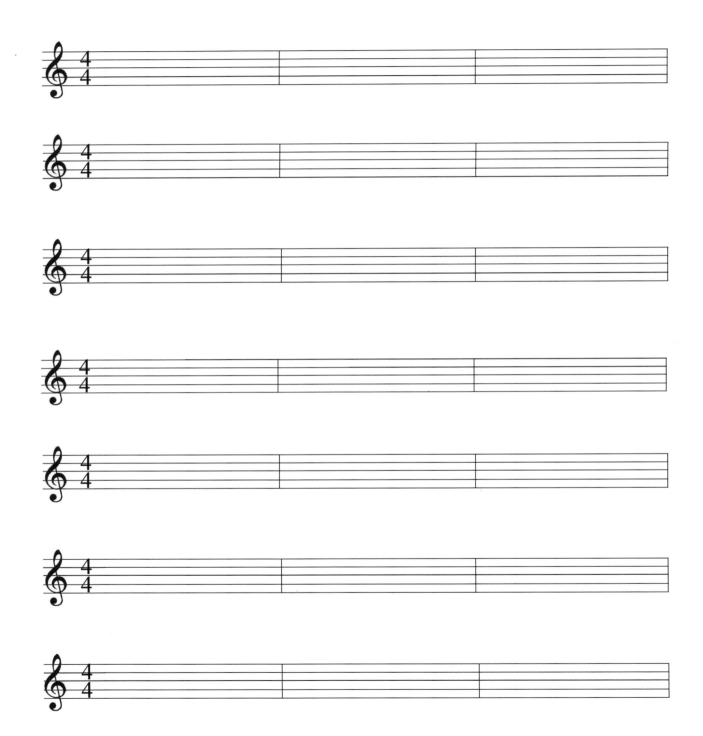

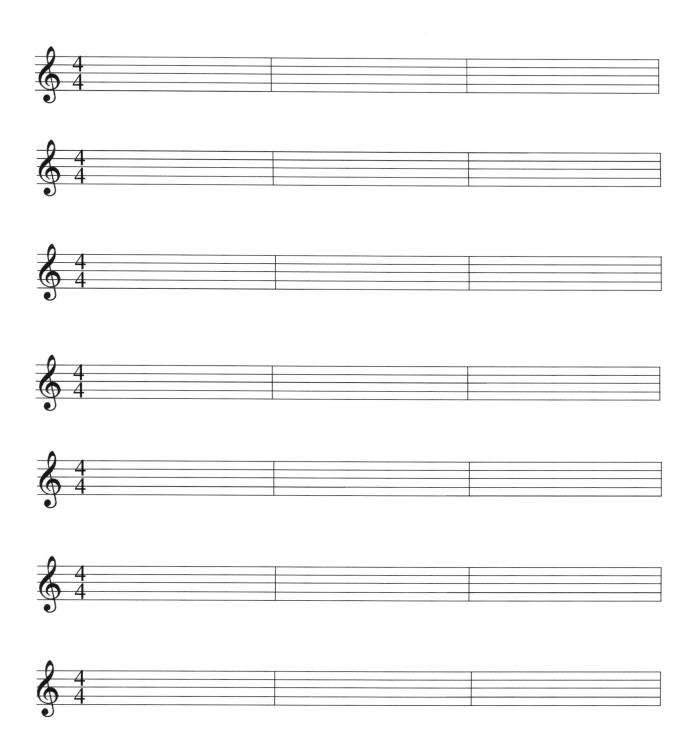

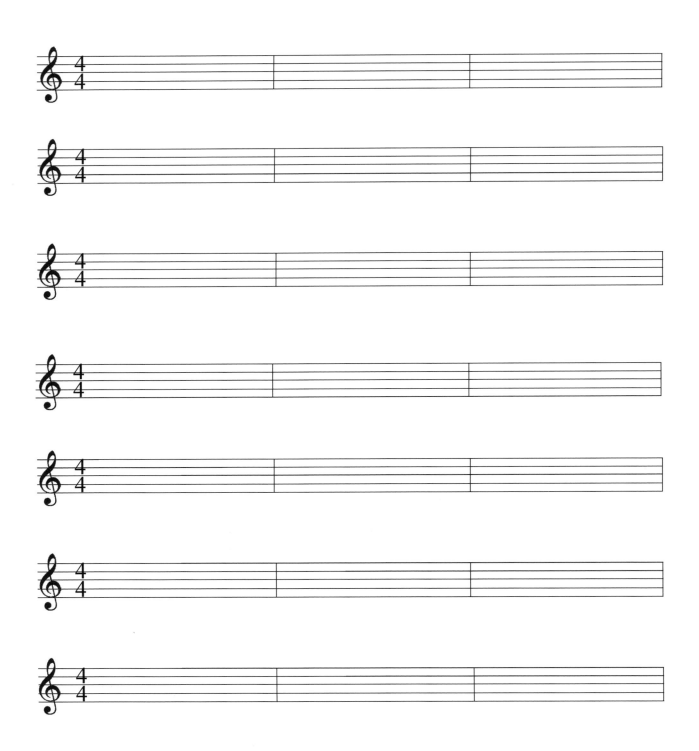

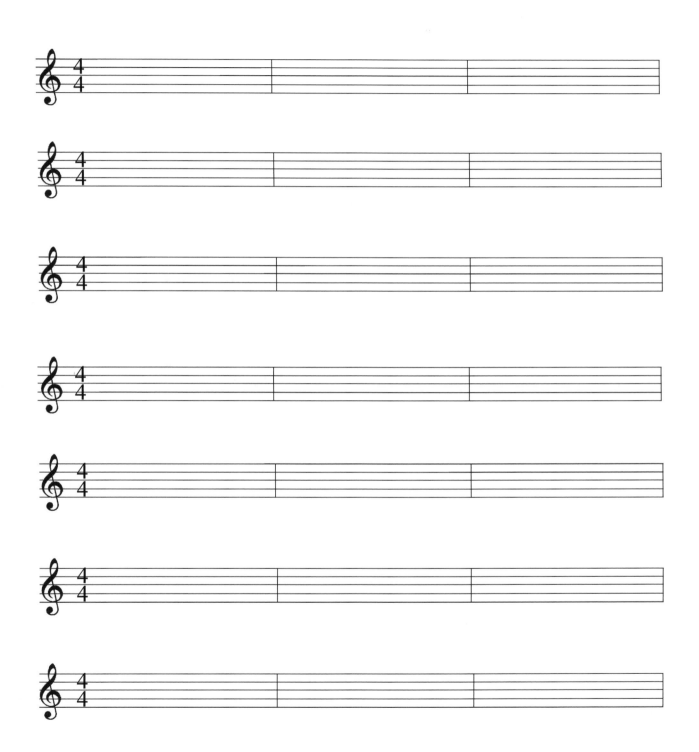

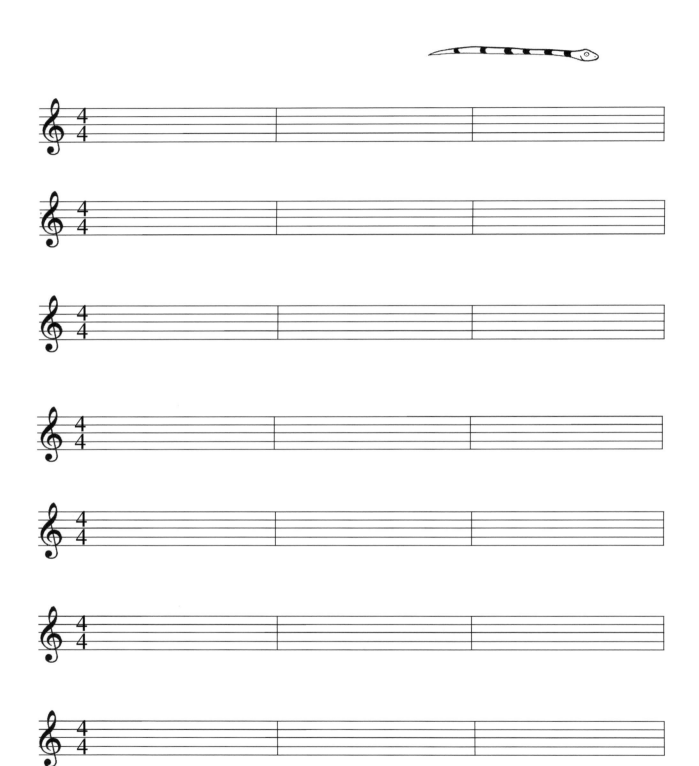

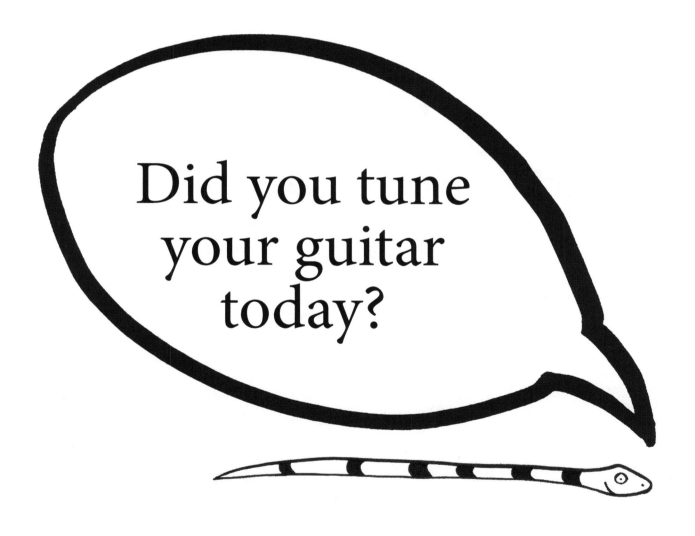

More Notes

The notes on the first position of the guitar

E A D G B E
6 5 4 3 2 1

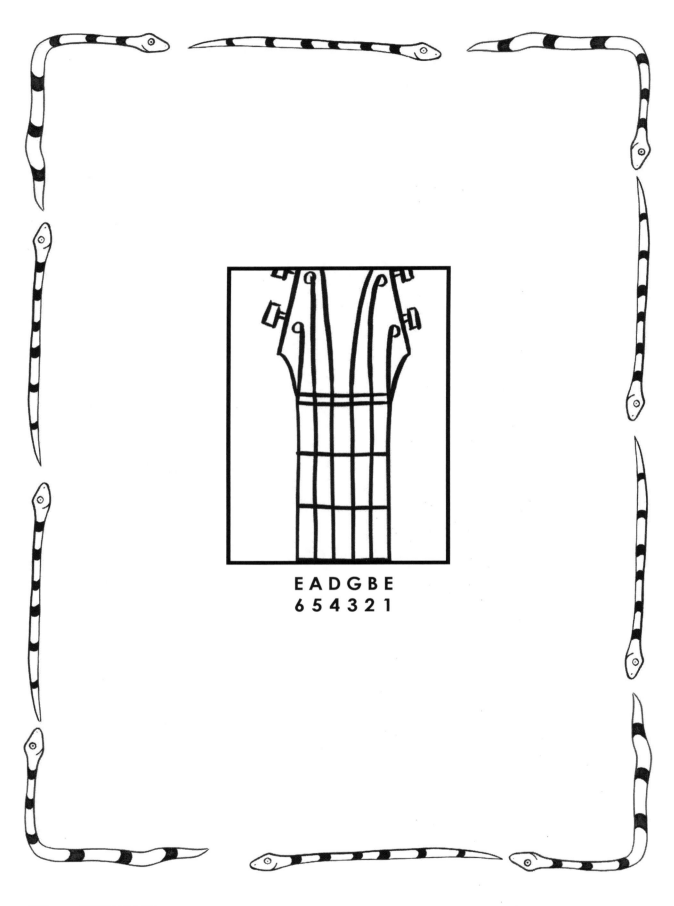

EADGBE
654321

E string: first string

E

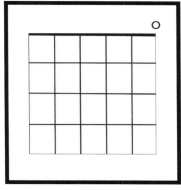

E NOTE

1st (E) STRING

0 FRET

0 FINGER

F

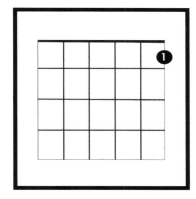

F NOTE

1st (E) STRING

1st FRET

1st FINGER

G

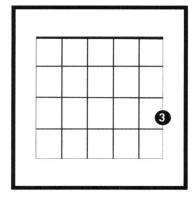
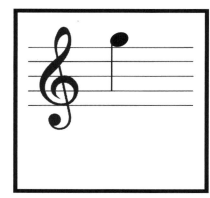

G NOTE

1st (E) STRING

3rd FRET

3rd FINGER

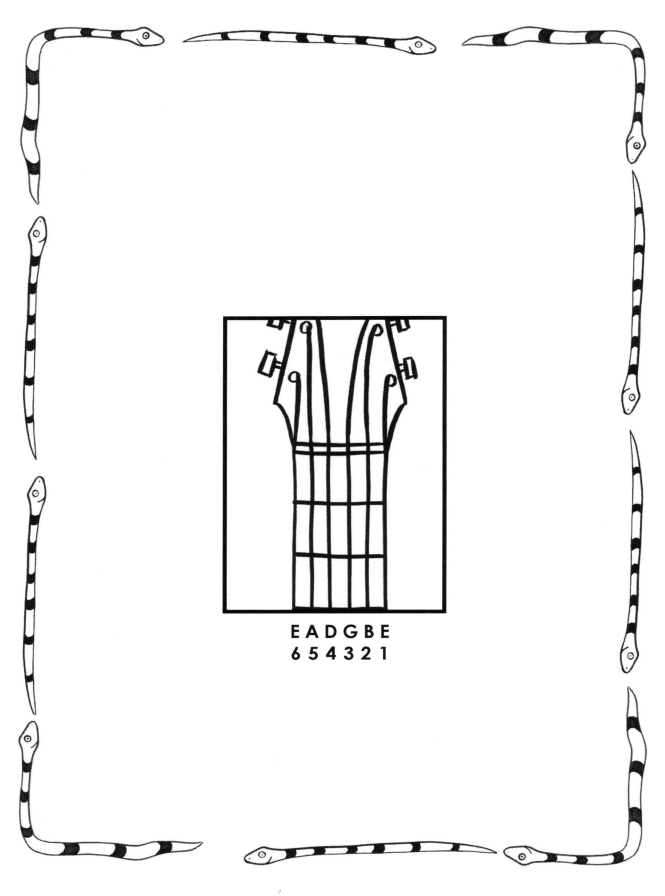

E A D G B E
6 5 4 3 2 1

B string: second string

B

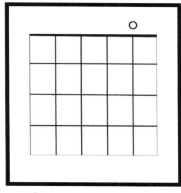 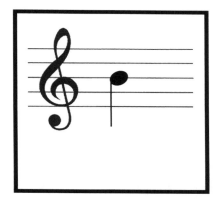

B NOTE

2nd (B) STRING

0 FRET

0 FINGER

C

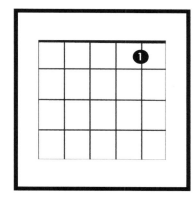 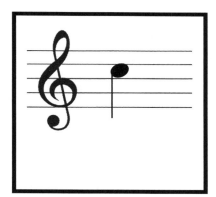

C NOTE

2nd (B) STRING

1st FRET

1st FINGER

D

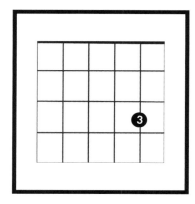 

D NOTE

2nd (B) STRING

3rd FRET

3rd FINGER

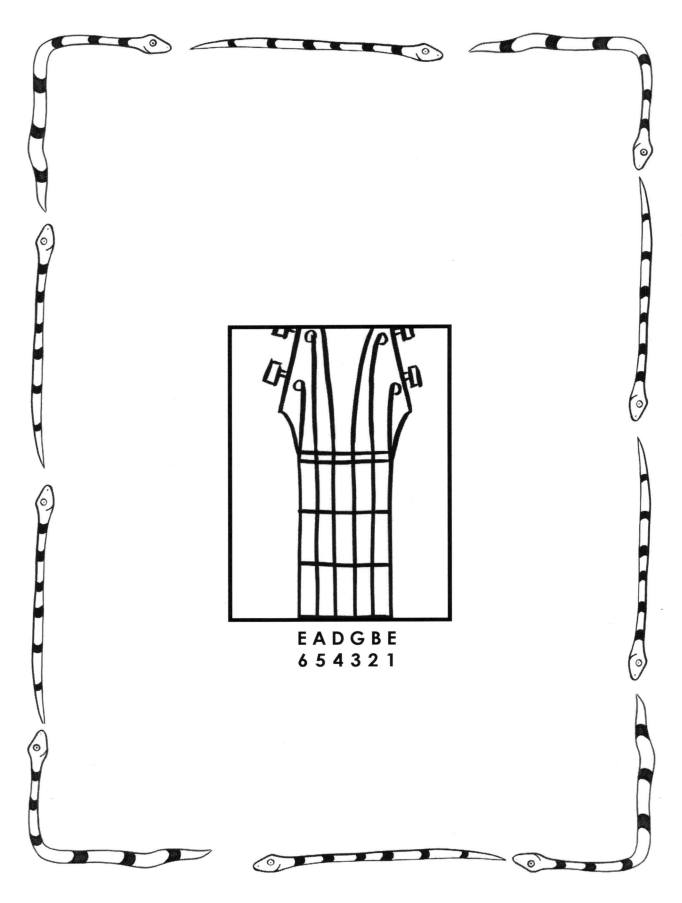

E A D G B E
6 5 4 3 2 1

G string: third string

G

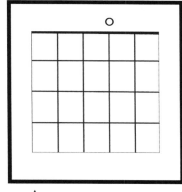

G NOTE

3rd (G) STRING

0 FRET

0 FINGER

A

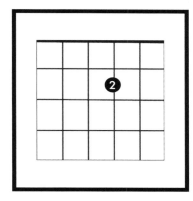

A NOTE

3rd (G) STRING

2nd FRET

2nd FINGER

You can do it!

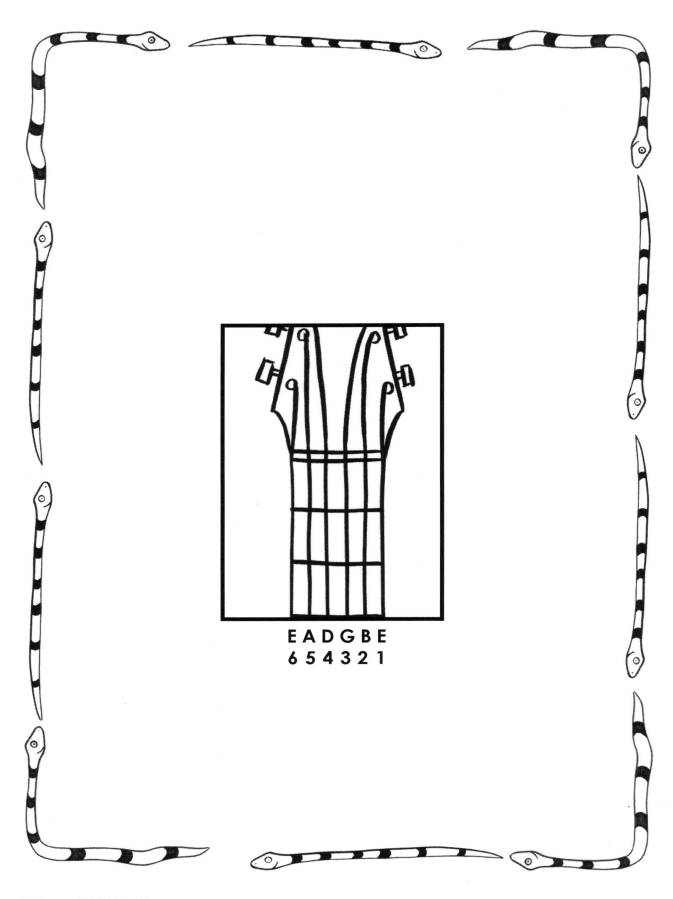

EADGBE
654321

D string: fourth string

D

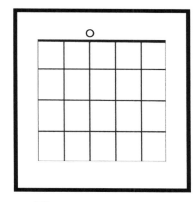

D NOTE

4th (D) STRING

0 FRET

0 FINGER

E

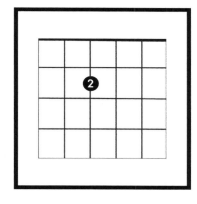
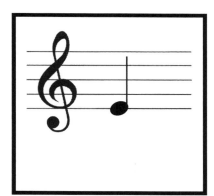

E NOTE

4th (D) STRING

2nd FRET

2nd FINGER

F

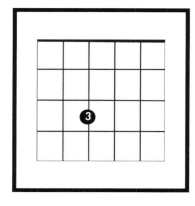

F NOTE

4th (D) STRING

3rd FRET

3rd FINGER

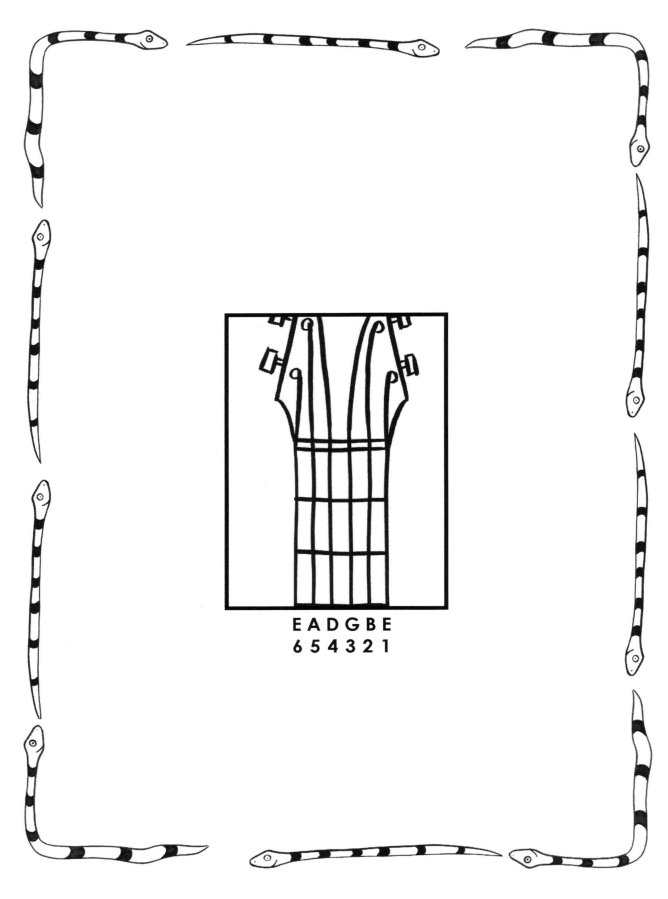

E A D G B E
6 5 4 3 2 1

A string: fifth string

A

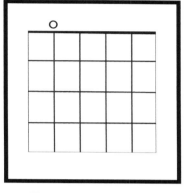
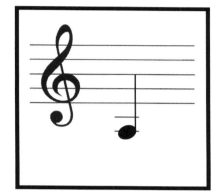

A NOTE

5th (A) STRING

0 FRET

0 FINGER

B

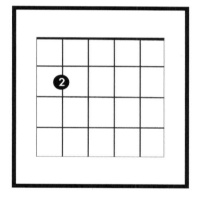

B NOTE

5th (A) STRING

2nd FRET

2nd FINGER

C

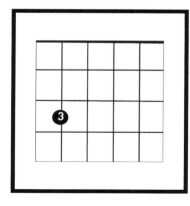
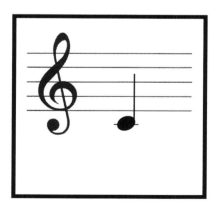

C NOTE

5th (A) STRING

3rd FRET

3rd FINGER

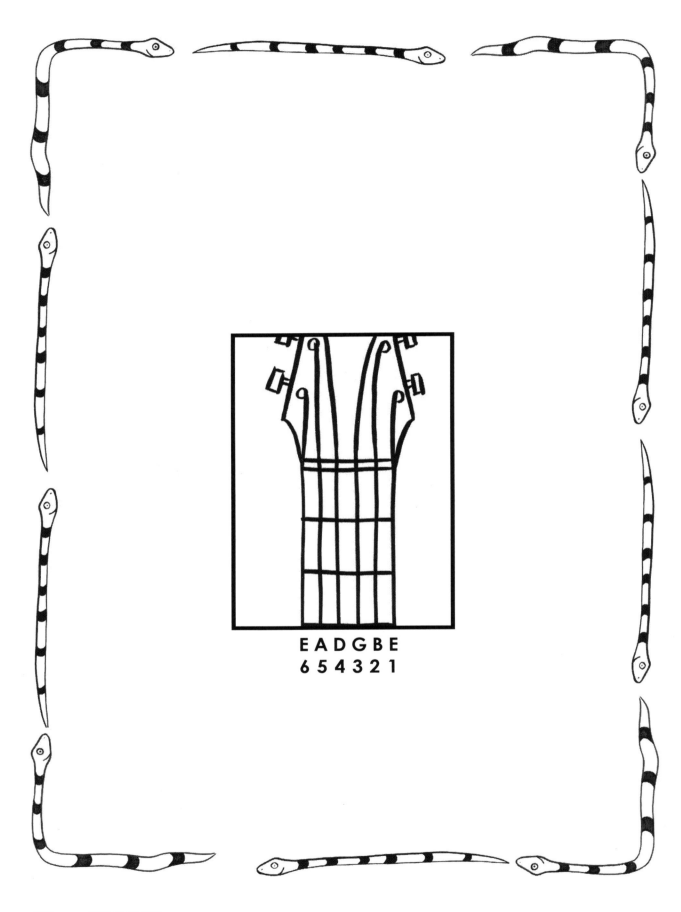

EADGBE
654321

E string (low): sixth string

E

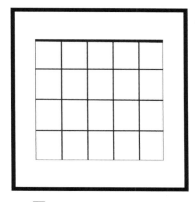 

E NOTE

6th (E) STRING

0 FRET

0 FINGER

F

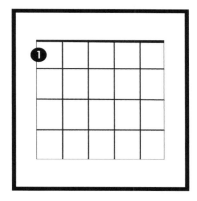 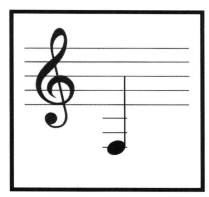

F NOTE

6th (E) STRING

1st FRET

1st FINGER

G

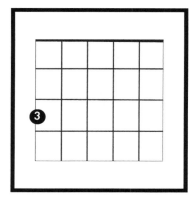 

G NOTE

6th (E) STRING

3rd FRET

3rd FINGER

Make up an exercise:

Write your own music with the three notes you learned how to play: **E**, **F** and **G** on page 105, and the notes on the other strings shown starting on page 217. You can use quarter notes, half notes, whole notes and rests. Remember, there are four beats per measure.

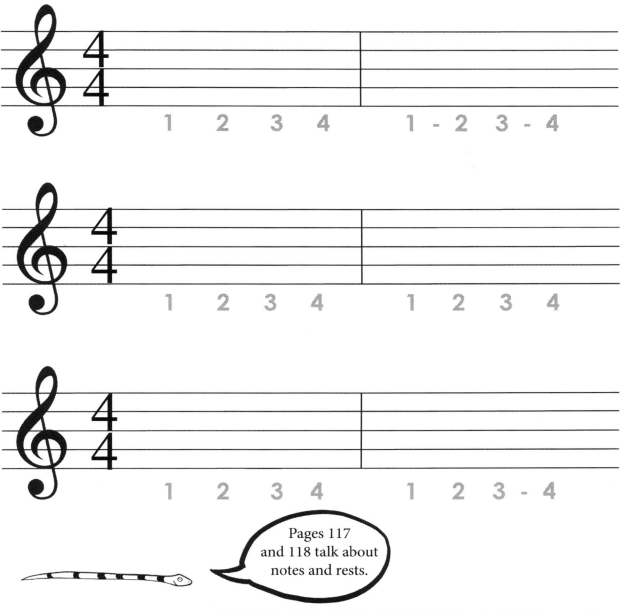

Pages 117 and 118 talk about notes and rests.

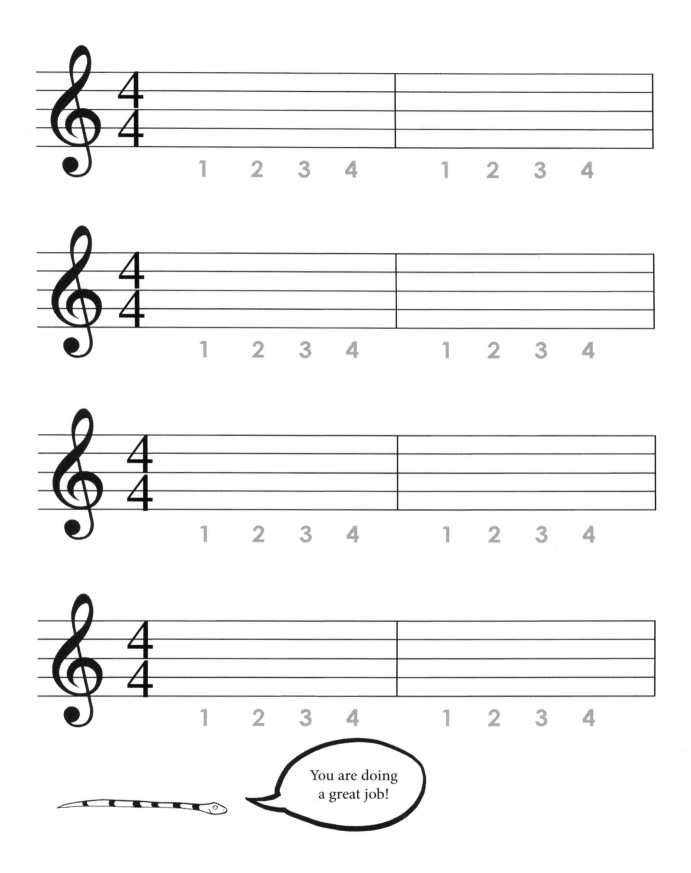

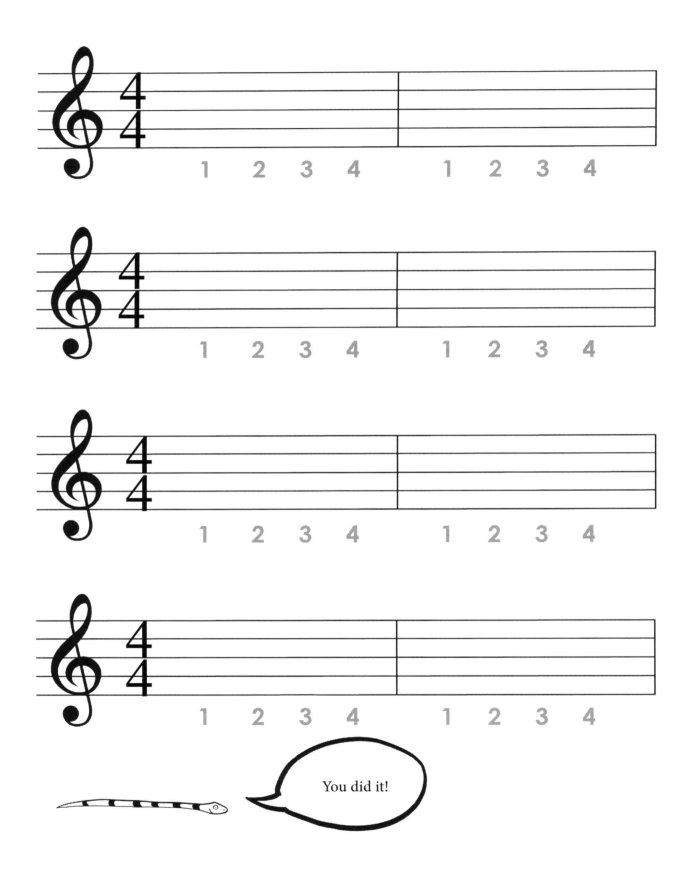

More Chords

More Chords

x = Don't play
o = Play Open

A

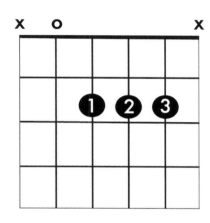

Am

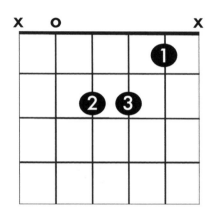

C

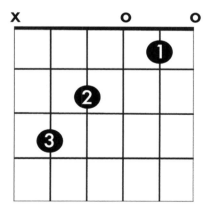

C7

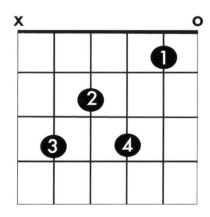

and more Chords

D

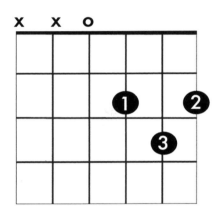

Dm

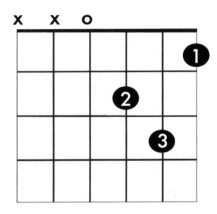

D7

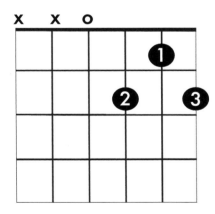

and more Chords

E

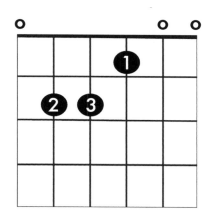

Em

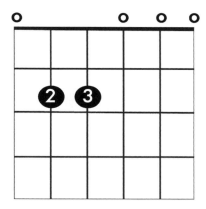

E7

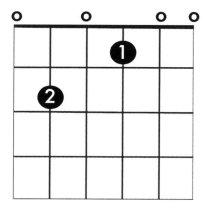

and more Chords

x = Don't play
o = Play Open

F

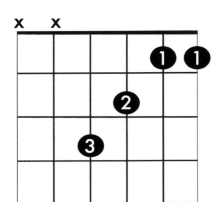

G

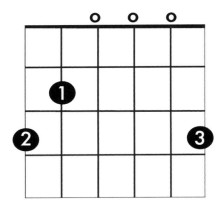

G7

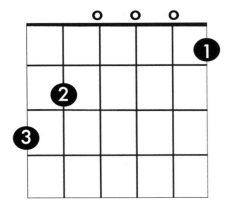

CHORD CHART

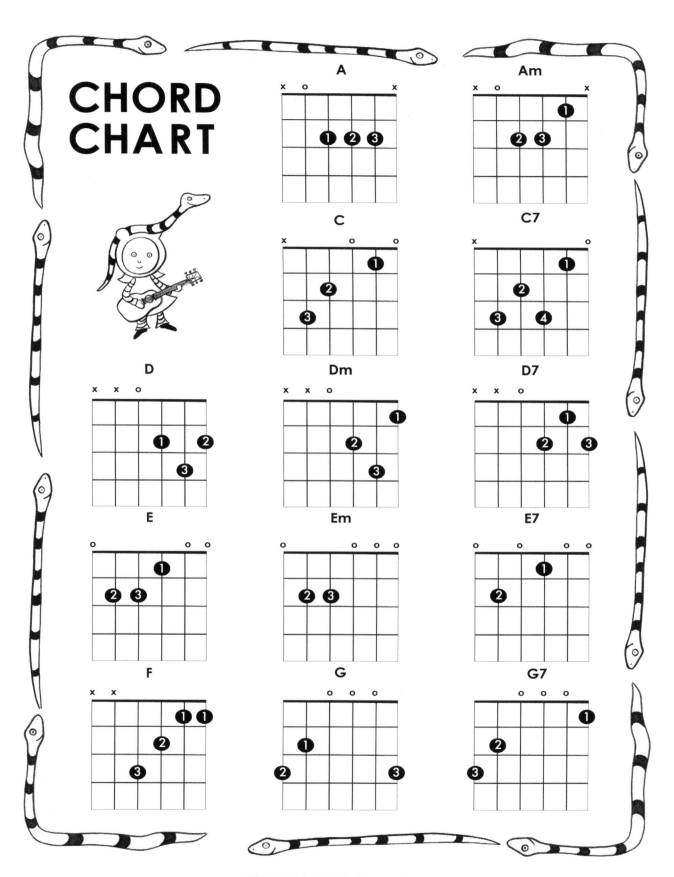

Fun songs to play!

Here are some fun songs to play.
The chords are taken from the chord
diagrams starting on page 235.
Make up your own strumming patterns.

G chord

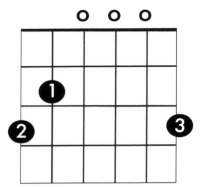

C chord

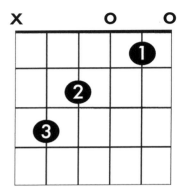

Em chord

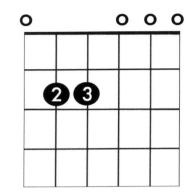

I Have a Pet Snake

Lyrics by Corey Klaus

G   C   Em
I have a pet snake - it has no arms or legs.

G   C   Em
I named it Squiggy because it likes to play.

Winden and Squiggy

Lyrics by Timber Hodges

G   C
Winden and Squiggy playing the guitar

Em   G
She wants to be a bear, a tree, and a rock star.

G chord

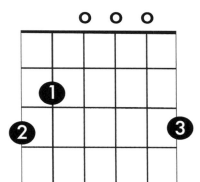

C chord

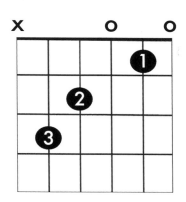

Em chord

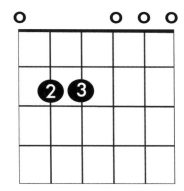

Squiggs is my Buddy Buddy

Lyrics by Corey Klaus

C   G
Squiggs is my buddy, buddy. Not some ruddy-duddy

Em   C
Follows me around when I go into town.

G
See him in a tree when he is hiding from me.

C
Tell him to get down when I make this sound.

C
Buddy-Buddy-Buddy, get down buddy,

G   C
Squiggy -iggy-iggs, get down from those twigs.

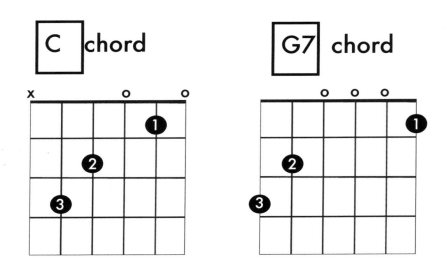

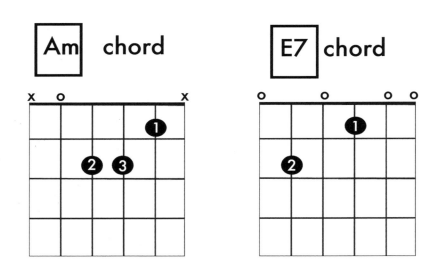

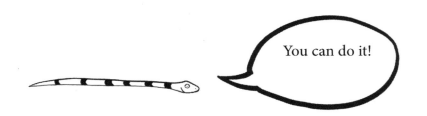

Three Little Kittens

Lyrics by Eliza Lee Cabot Follen

VERSE 1

<u>C</u>
Three little kittens they lost their mittens,

       <u>G7</u>   <u>C</u>
And they began to cry,

Oh, mother dear, we sadly fear,

      <u>G7</u>   <u>C</u>
Our mittens we have lost.

   <u>Am</u>
What! Lost your mittens, you naughty kittens!

   <u>E7</u>   <u>Am</u>
Then you shall have no pie.

<u>G7</u>   <u>C</u>   <u>G7</u>   <u>C</u>
Meow, meow, meow, meow, meow, meow, meow.

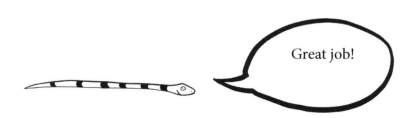

Great job!

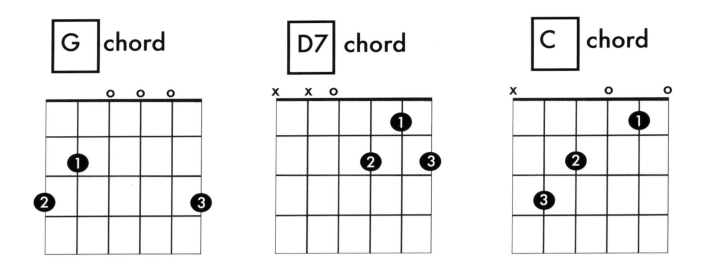

G chord   D7 chord   C chord

Hey Diddle Diddle

G   **D7**
Hey, diddle, diddle, the cat and the fiddle

G   **D7**
The cow jumped over the moon.

    C   **G**
The little dog laughed to see such sport

    D7   **G**
And the dish ran away with the spoon.

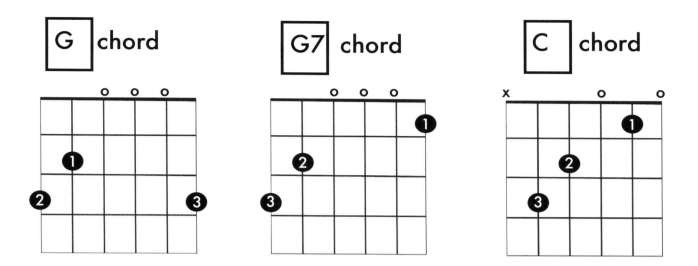

Twinkle, Twinkle, Little Star

Lyrics by Jane Taylor

<u>G</u>
Twinkle, twinkle little star

<u>G7</u>   <u>G</u>   <u>C</u>
How I wonder what you are

<u>C</u>   <u>G</u>
Up above the world so high.

<u>C</u>   <u>G</u>
Like a diamond in the sky.

<u>C</u>
Twinkle, twinkle little star

<u>C</u>   <u>G</u>
How I wonder what you are.

Have fun!

Squiggy and I had so much fun learning to play the guitar with you! I hope we can play together again soon.

xo
Winden and Squiggy

Remember to practice!

Make it fun and pass it along.
Teach your friends your favorite song!
Play for your folks.
Play for your snake.
But please don't forget to
play for yourself,
for goodness sake!

Corey Klaus

Danielle Almond

Corey Klaus has been sharing his love of music and teaching all over southeastern Pennsylvania for the last decade. He has worked closely with music therapists and on various projects, honing his skills for working with children and helping them learn music on their level.

Squiggy

Danielle Almond

Squiggy the snake is named after Squiggy the dog. Squiggy would like to learn how to play the guitar; however, he is not sure how to use his paws to play chords. He enjoys listening to music, eating, and watching television, when he is not chasing cats.

Pamela Hodges

Jeremy Cowart

Pamela Hodges is an artist and writer. She writes about art and creativity at her blog, pamelahodges. com, to help you create the art you dream about. Pamela is also the typist for her cat, Harper, who writes about life as a cat at thecatwhowrites.com.

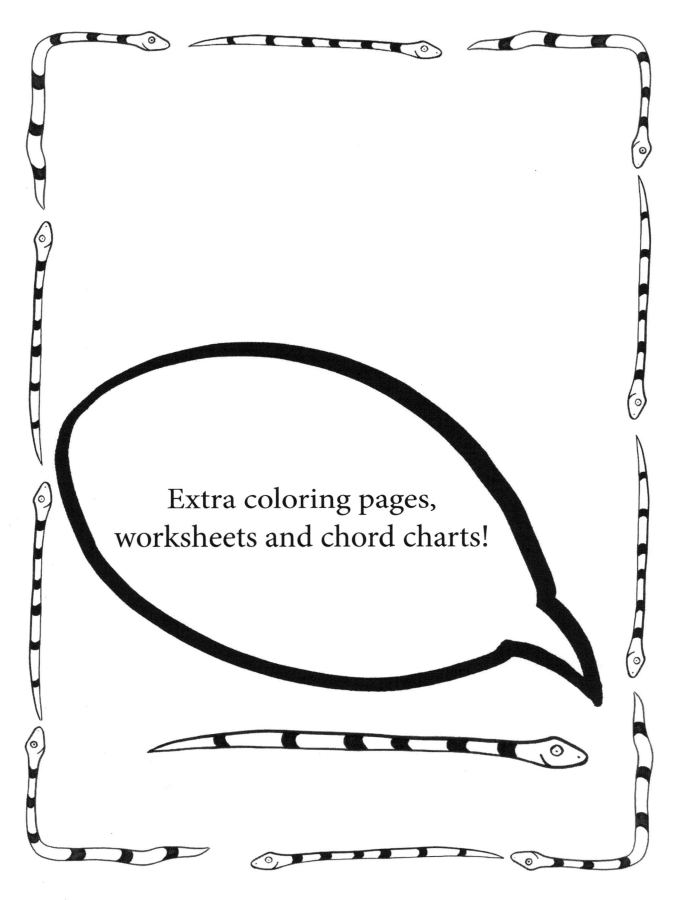

Extra coloring pages, worksheets and chord charts!

COLOR THE GUITAR
DRAW A DESIGN!

COLOR THE GUITAR
DRAW A DESIGN!

COLOR THE GUITAR
DRAW A DESIGN!

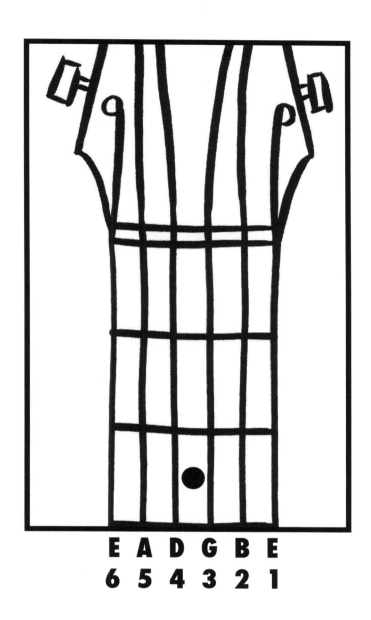

E A D G B E
6 5 4 3 2 1

Elephants **A**nd **D**onkeys **G**row **B**ig **E**ars

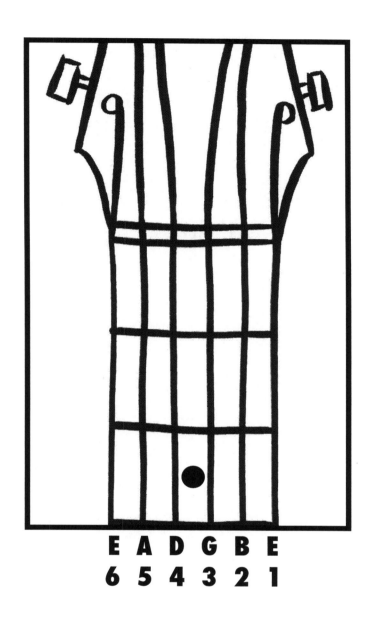

Elephants
And
Donkeys
Grow
Big
Ears

E A D G B E
6 5 4 3 2 1

Elephants **A**nd **D**onkeys **G**row **B**ig **E**ars

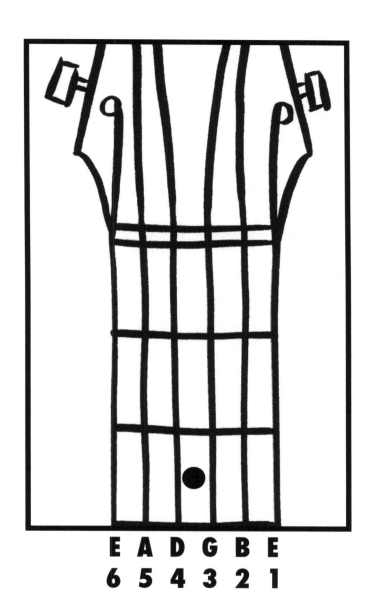

Elephants
And
Donkeys
Grow
Big
Ears

E A D G B E
6 5 4 3 2 1

Elephants **A**nd **D**onkeys **G**row **B**ig **E**ars

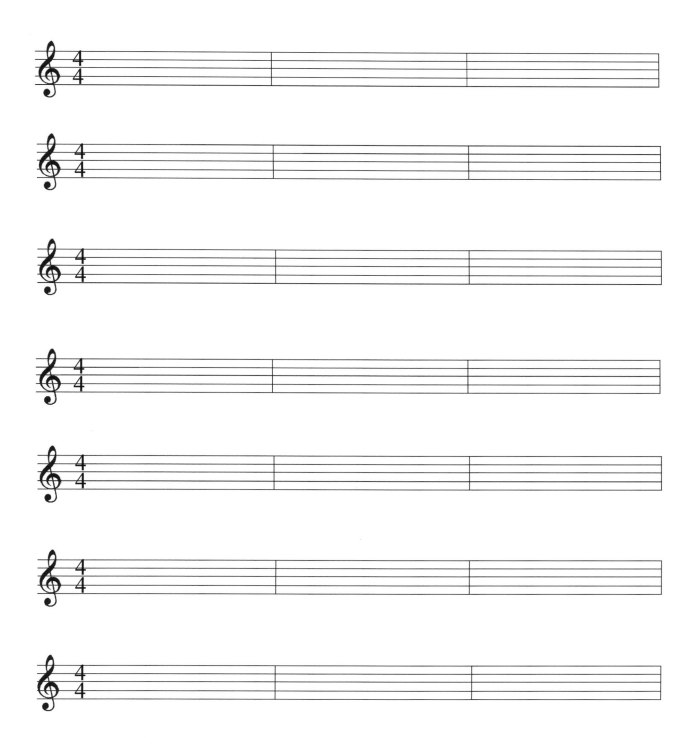

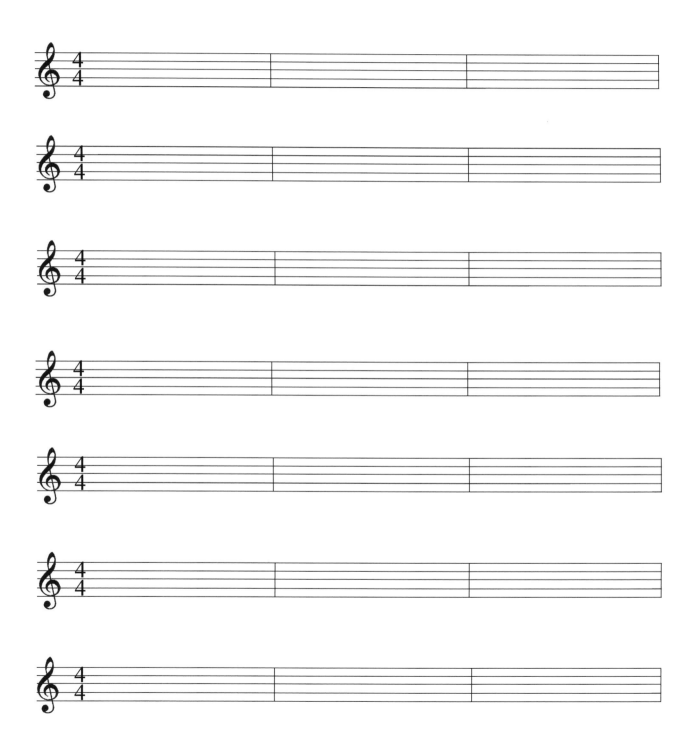

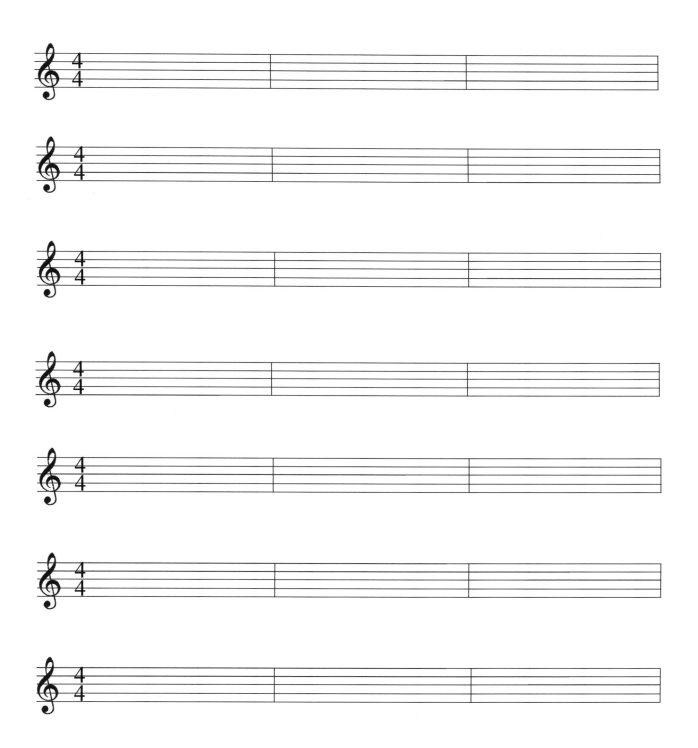

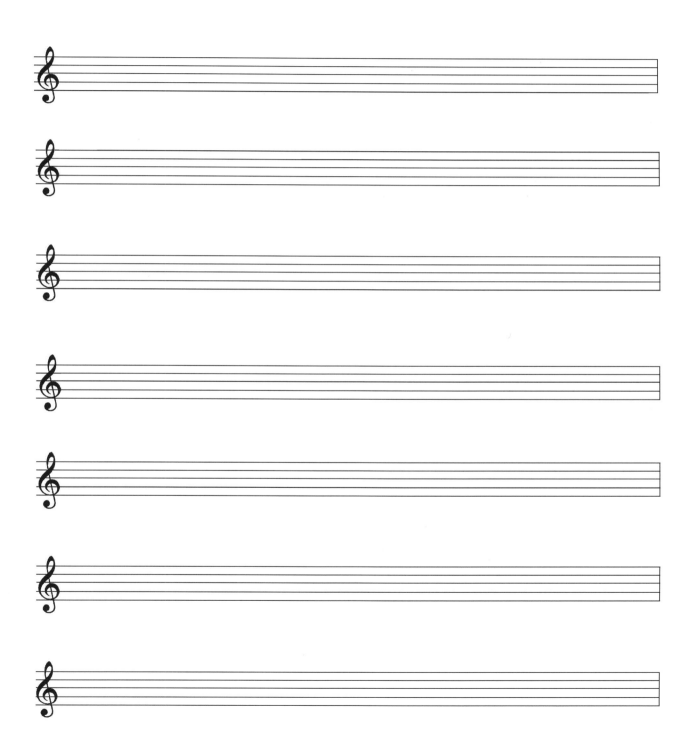

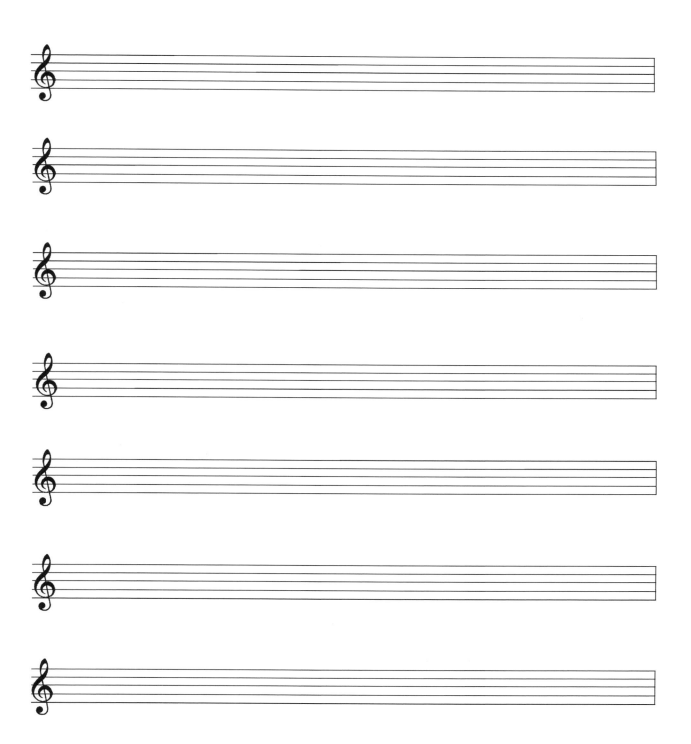

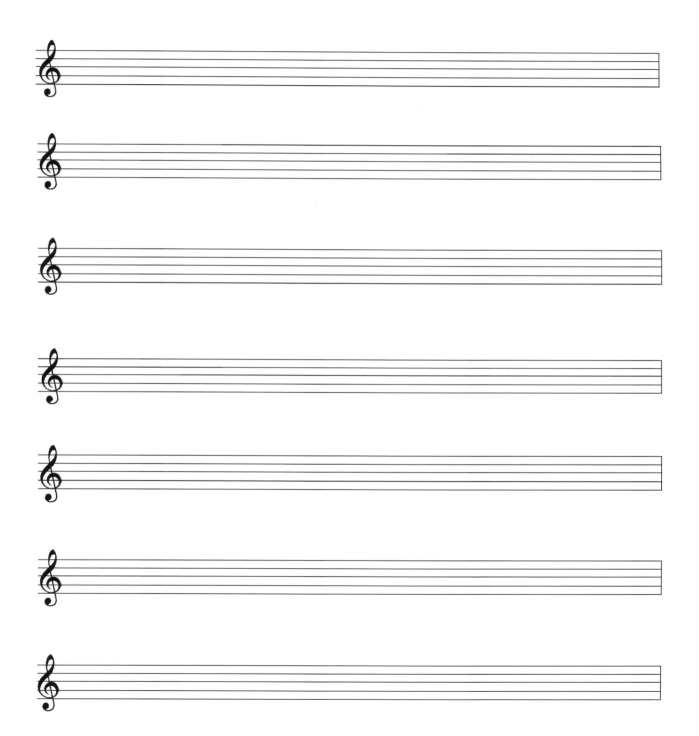

CHORD CHART

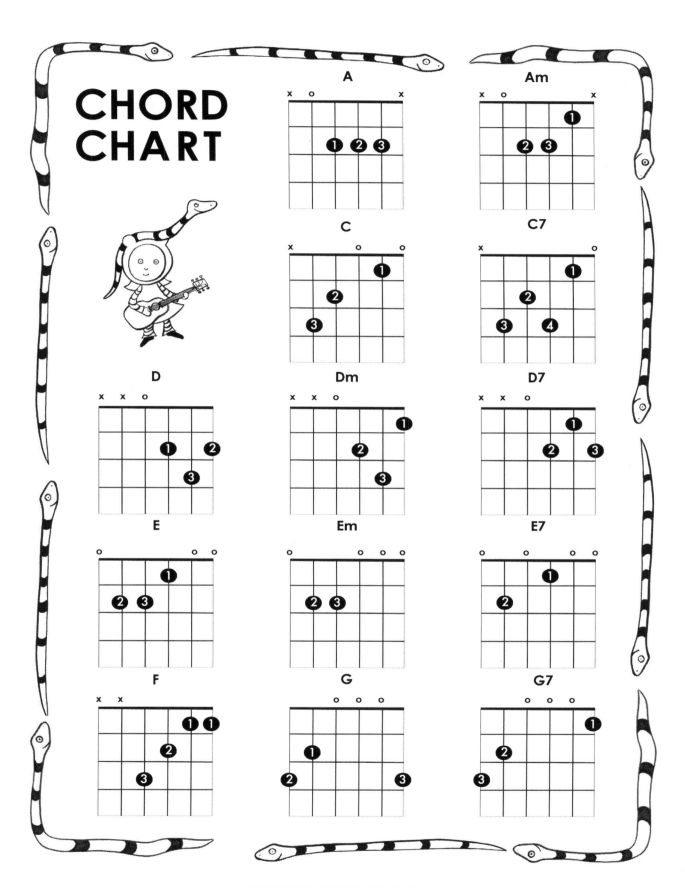

CHORD CHART

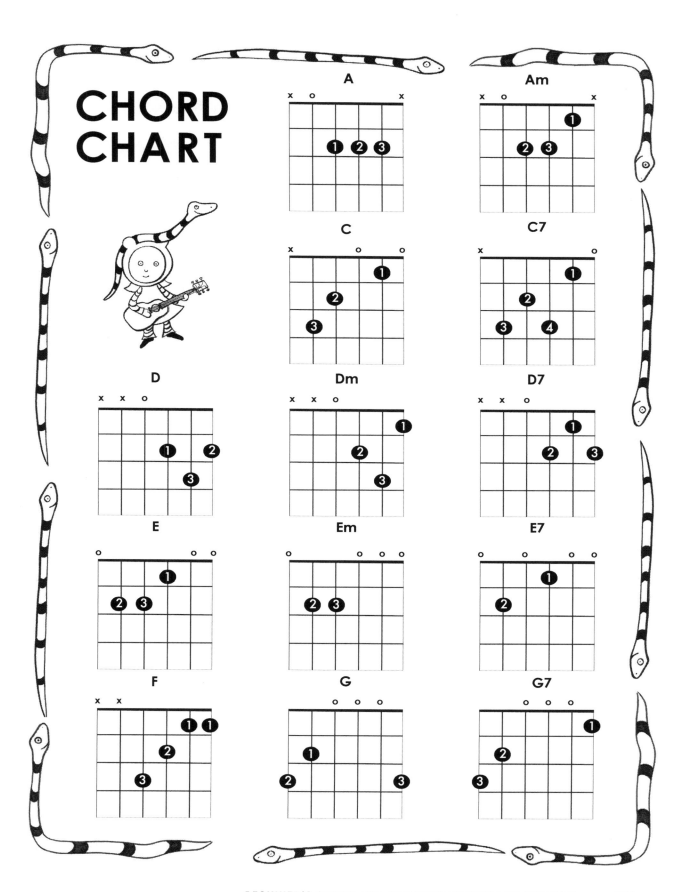

CHORD CHART

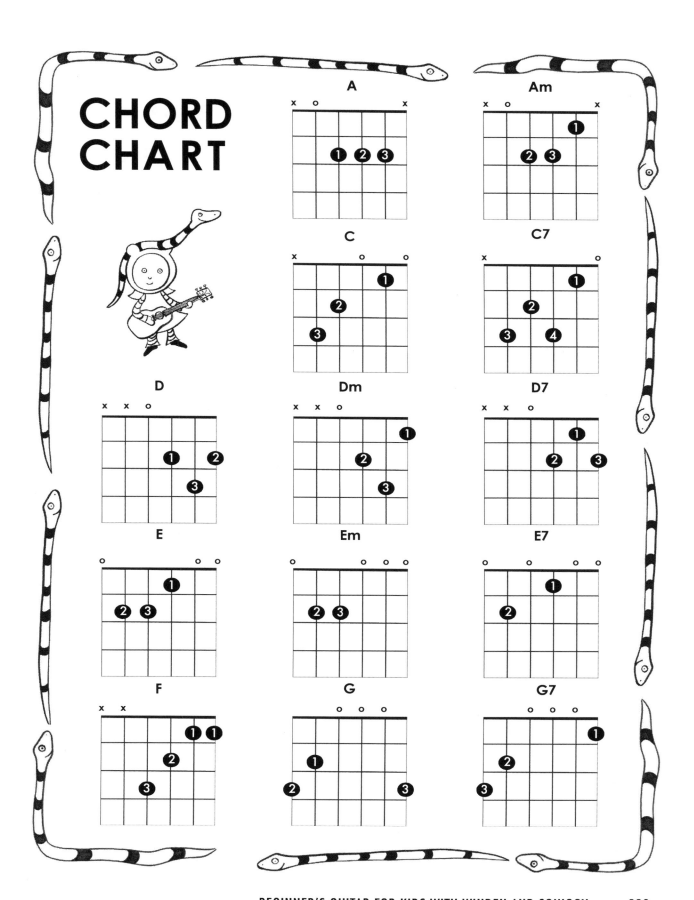

Made in the USA
San Bernardino, CA
15 April 2020